MINDSET FOR MASTERY

MINDSET *for* MASTERY

AN NFL CHAMPION'S GUIDE TO
REACHING YOUR GREATNESS

RYAN HARRIS

LIONCREST

PUBLISHING

MINDSET FOR MASTERY

An NFL Champion's Guide to Reaching Your Greatness

ISBN   978-1-5445-1059-0 *Hardcover*

       978-1-5445-1057-6 *Paperback*

       978-1-5445-1058-3 *Ebook*

I dedicate this book to you, your mindset, and the beyond you create.

CONTENTS

INTRODUCTION

My journey to becoming a Super Bowl champion was never easy.

As a kid, I was chubby. I was made fun of all the time in school. I felt out of place. The only thing that made me feel normal was football. I loved watching the game because there were big guys like me on the field.

I could not wait for my chance to play.

In eighth grade, my chance arrived. I was happy because I was finally in a situation where I thought that my size and "want to" would give me purpose and use. I was the most excited kid on that field to have a helmet, shoulder pads, and cleats. I thought, "Now I'm going to be a real football player."

Then we got our pads.

When we were given our gear that first day, one of my buddies said to me, "Hey, let's go heads up." Despite the fact that I was so excited to have my very own helmet and shoulder pads, I said no. My friend kept pestering me, "Come on, let's go heads up." I continued to say no and made excuses for not wanting to, but he was not buying my answers. He wanted a concrete reason. Finally, he dragged it out of me. "All right," I said. "But you can't tell anybody...I don't know what 'heads up' means; I don't know how to hit."

The loudest laughter I had ever heard roared from his mouth.

Everyone turned to look. My now onetime friend was causing a scene out of my worst nightmares. He screamed to everyone, "Ryan doesn't know how to hit!" I hung my head, completely embarrassed. I felt big. Awkward. Useless. There I was, being laughed at by every single member of the team. Even some of the coaches were snickering. They were confused. How does this big kid not know how to hit?

The truth was, I had dreamed about the day I would be able to suit up and walk out onto a football field as a player, but I never actually used my pads.

The next practice, it took everything in me just to show up. I stood by myself away from the team before practice started—or did they all stay away from me? Regardless, I was determined to become a football player.

Three plays into practice, one of the kids made an interception. He came flying down the sideline. I ran toward him, closed my eyes, and put all the fear, embarrassment, awkwardness, and ignorance into one thrust as I hoped I would make my first "hit."

I knocked the shit out of him.

Turns out, I knew how to hit after all. No one laughed anymore. All of a sudden, it was good to be big. I was more than some chubby kid. I could protect whoever had the ball. I could move someone to create an opportunity for my team. In that way, football loved me first, and I was incredibly grateful and willing to do anything to keep that feeling alive.

That was the first day I chose my mindset.

If I believe anything to be true today, it is that the right mindset, the right practices, and perseverance create success no matter who you are. As a ten-year veteran of the NFL and a Super Bowl champion, I know that mindset makes all the difference between being ordinary and extraordinary. From the first time I suited up as a young boy to stepping onto the field at Notre Dame to being drafted in the NFL in 2007, I have had to face obstacle after obstacle. I have persevered through three back surgeries, five surgeries to save my lower leg, and a crippling toe injury. I have had to prove myself on five different NFL teams and have been let go throughout my career before becoming a Super Bowl 50 champion.

The lessons I learned on the field are lessons I have applied to life. These are the lessons I want to share with you so you, too, can have the mindset that creates a life of joy.

No matter who you are or where you have been, we all share similar experiences in life. We all experience pain, loss, gain, embarrassment, and paying taxes. We all have similar thoughts.

"I can't."

"It's too hard."

"It will take too much time."

"I failed."

"No one else has to work this hard."

Everyone experiences fear, self-doubt, and embarrassment, but how you approach and attack these feelings determines your success and your capabilities.

Far too often, we allow these thoughts to prevent us from living our wildest dreams. Your thoughts regarding whatever opportunity lies ahead of you are an example of what *can* happen. If you think it will be too hard, it will be too hard. If you think it will take too much time, it will. These self-limiting thoughts come in all shapes and sizes. If you let them in, they will tear your dreams apart. However, if you refuse to listen, you can achieve anything.

I wrote this book to share with you how mindset has worked in my life. How my failures are as common as the next champion's. And how you can create your mindset through thick and thin to achieve your greatness.

I am not going to lie to you: choosing your mindset will not be easy. I am here to tell you, however, that you *can* do it. It takes time and a lot of failure. Choosing your mindset in the best and worst times will enable you to master your achievements, goals, and dreams. When you embark on the path of creating your mindset, you have chosen a mindset for mastery. In fact, by picking up this book, you are already on your way.

THE CHAMPION WITHIN YOU

In this book, you are going to find the ability you already have within you to achieve greatness. It is through the mindset of mastery that every successful person has overcome self-limiting thoughts about their life and career, and it is what I want to teach you in this book.

Once you harness your beliefs, your mindset will create your wildest dreams as you visualize the prize (chapter two), pick up a shovel and dig (chapter three), persevere (chapter four), invest your time (chapter five), succeed through self-care (chapter six), look to the beyond in mastery (chapter seven), lead like a leader (chapter eight), and celebrate your every win (chapter nine). I want you to feel how powerful it is to create a mindset where you are willing to fail to succeed. When you strive for a mindset of mastery, you gain a perspective to overcome obstacles you previously could not imagine overcoming.

You may be a CEO of a major company who lost gratitude and zeal for life; *you can go beyond*. You can create more with your mindset.

You may be a student who is struggling through your classes, but you know there is more inside of you; *you can go beyond*.

You may be a mid-level employee, or a weekend warrior searching for yourself; go beyond and *choose* your mindset.

You become a champion the moment you choose your mindset. And when you choose your mindset, you choose to change the world.

So let's change the world.

CHAPTER ONE

I Am, I Can, I Will

"I am the greatest, I said that even before I knew I was."

—MUHAMMAD ALI

We all face self-doubt. We doubt whether we have the talent. We doubt our choices. At times we even doubt who we are. We wonder whether we have what it takes to get the job, the house, the relationship we desire. All these doubts are normal. In achieving your greatness, you face the choice to overcome them.

One of the best ways I have found to move past self-doubt are the phrases *I am, I can, I will*. These statements will give you a belief in yourself to do what you truly want and create a foundation for success. With these phrases, you can build a mindset that negates the fears and doubts you have had at every turn in life.

Muhammad Ali's words are powerful to me because the first time I read them was the first time I had heard a champion talk about self-doubt. Before then, I looked at great achievers like Ali and thought, "They must've always known they were great." But reading that quote and knowing that one of the greatest champions of the world did not believe he was the greatest at some point? That gave me relief. It made me see that I was not the only one facing self-doubt. And neither are you. If you worry about being smart enough, financially savvy enough, or talented enough, then you are not alone. Self-doubt can be found at every turn of events in your life, but that does not mean you have to give up on your goals.

No matter what anyone, even that nagging voice in your head, says, you can believe in yourself. The moment where you believe in yourself before anybody else does will be powerful and necessary to achieving your dreams. *I am, I can, I will* creates the mindset of doing something in the face of adversity. These words give you confidence to try something new. They highlight opportunity in your life in real time. They create and reinforce a mindset to reach your goals instead of focusing on your doubts.

I AM

The moment where you can say *I am* _____ and mean it, you embody self-belief.

The night before the Super Bowl, I said to myself, "*I am* a world champion." I was not a Super Bowl champion at that point in time. I was just a football player with eight years of previous failure and a dream. I did not want to limit myself by thinking that I was not a champion simply because it had not happened yet. So I said to myself, "*I am* a champion," before I even stepped onto that field, before I was ever able to hold that trophy. I believed in my opportunity the next day, and I believed that all the work I had put in made me ready to become a champion, but arriving at that point was literally back-breaking at times.

Thousands of dreams come to a terrified halt before belief in the self is achieved. Too often, people become stuck in the idea that if something terrifies them, they are not supposed to do it. Or if they do not feel they are good enough right away, they will stop as well. It amazes me that people feel they *should* be good at something and, when they encounter the first bump in the road, they crumble.

I see this all the time in parenting. Parents tell everyone how good their child is at sports, even when they are only six years old. Yet the moment the kid gets to high school, encounters someone better than them, or encounters loss of any kind, they collapse.

So many people now do not expect to be terrified, embarrassed, or bad on the way to success, but these feelings are all part of achievement. They will happen, and when they do, good. Instead of collapsing into your fear, find the work you can do, and start by finding yourself. Use the phrase *I am* to get yourself there.

I have used *I am* so much it has touched every aspect of my life.

I am a new parent and have no idea what I am doing.

I am getting ready to meet Barack Obama in the White House.

I am a broadcaster and we are going live for the first time in 3...2...1...

I am standing at the altar to be married to the most epic, awesome person in the world.

I am on vacation and *I am* not checking email.

I am grateful...

On and on we go!

The words *I am* give you the space to recognize and build resolve around your identity. The words *I am* give you a moment of self-awareness. They create a moment to be honest with yourself. No matter if you are terrified or ecstatic.

I am good enough!

I am frustrated.

I am distracted.

I am getting closer to my goal!

The words *I am* also help you take ownership of the negative.

I am not working hard enough. *I am* being lazy. *I am* not listening.

That same night before the Super Bowl, I said to myself, "*I am* terrified that my greatest achievement will be my greatest failure if we lose this game."

When you speak the words *I am*, you take stock of who you are and where you are. You take stock of what you are feeling. You become empowered by your identity. And you are now ready to take meaningful action with a confidence and entirety that your mindset has built. Champions know this as flow. With the words *I am*, you create total resolve. You know who you are and the why behind the moment you find yourself in. With this identity, honesty, and resolve, you will feel the freedom to move forward.

I CAN

"Likewise in painting, I can do all things."

—LEONARDO DA VINCI

The statement *I can* creates a willingness to take action in even the darkest moments of your journey. At some point, your *good* will not be good enough. Let me repeat: at some point your *good* will not be good enough.

In those moments, instead of looking to blame someone else, speak the words *I can* to find the opportunities in front of you. Even if you do not believe you have the ability, you immediately instill a willingness that highlights opportunity. That willingness convinces others, even if not yourself, of your ability.

If you say, "*I am* (your name here). I have not been performing the way I wanted to. *I can* change that. *I can* go to bed earlier. *I can* eat better. *I can* try something new," you create a willingness. When you say *I can*, you create change.

The power of *I can* saved my career.

After four years in the NFL, I had a coach who wanted me to improve. He wanted me to learn new plays, try new drills. But I was in a place of heightened importance and arrogance and thought, "I don't have to do that! I know what I'm doing. I've started twenty-two games in the NFL; I don't need to be taught this. I don't need to learn anything new." I had already earned incredible success and I was unwilling to change. Because of that mindset, I was released. Fired.

I did not respect the opportunity I had, and my attitude was palpable. The coaches noticed that mentality, and they did not want a guy like me around. Who would? I will never forget that day. The day I was called upstairs and had to return to the locker room to gather my things. The air in the room dropped out. I was caught completely by surprise. I was so embarrassed. Everyone knew that something must have happened for me to lose my job. That I did not do something correctly. I was terrified of what would happen next. How would I tell people I was arrogant and lost my job? How would I explain to my wife in our first year of marriage that I had failed and was now unemployed?

All these thoughts went around and around as I drove away from the Denver Broncos facility with tears in my eyes, my hands shaking in disbelief.

And there in that moment, I had a choice to make. I could

choose to wallow in my embarrassment, pain, and unemployment. Or I could move forward and let this be the beginning of a new page. Let this be wherever the beyond took me.

In choosing to move forward, I said the words *I can*.

I can turn this experience into one of the greatest moments of my career.

I can work harder than before.

I can be grateful for the fact that *I can* drive home to my wife because *I am* a husband.

I can stop by my favorite fast food restaurant on the way home.

Immediately my spirits lifted. Immediately I had new options that did not exist in my career before being let go. And when I went to bed that night happy, laughing with my wife, stuffed after eating my feelings, I understood the power of *I can*.

And wouldn't you know it. That very next morning after being released, I signed with the Houston Texans. Coached by Gary Kubiak, the very same man I would win a Super Bowl with three years later in a triumphant return to the Denver Broncos because of my willingness to work, play, learn, and fail.

My greatest failure built a willingness I did not have.

Before thinking about any result or having any expectation, create your willingness by saying *I can*. Your willingness will carry you further than you could ever expect. *I can* brings you to new experiences, new people, new contacts, new foods, or a new hobby. *I can* leads to enjoyment, community, and connection.

When you speak the words *I can,* you keep moving, you keep believing, and then, you are led to action.

I WILL

To crystalize your belief and complete your mindset, you must take one final step.

Speak the words *I will.*

I will becomes the commitment to your self-awareness, identity, and willingness. *I will* places the motion behind your commitment to your dreams.

I am bad at money; *I can* change that. *I will* reach out to my frugal friend. *I will* search the web for financial literacy advocates and podcasts to listen to. *I will* look them up now. *I will* listen during my car rides.

I am a Muslim. *I can* overcome other people's bias, to build strong communities. *I will* interact with those different than me. *I will* give people the benefit of the doubt. *I will* join an interfaith dialogue group to learn and teach.

I am terrified the night before the Super Bowl that my greatest accomplishment will be my greatest failure. *I can* wake up in the morning, put my pads on, and knock the crap outta someone. *I will.*

Immediately after saying, "I am, I can, I will," you take action. You feel your identity. You see yourself achieve these goals. And you do it.

You begin to see how *I am, I can, I will* can be applied to all aspects of life.

Too many people say, "I want to be great. I want to be rich. I want to be wealthy." But rarely do people state them as goals. Rarely are they willing to do the work to make what they want happen.

Not you. Not anymore.

Stating your goals and where you want to be can make

your actions powerful, but we are often not encouraged to say them out loud. We do not even talk about them in our daily conversations. Do you think we had a goal the year we won the Super Bowl? You betcha. Could we have won the Super Bowl without stating our goals? Hell no.

You have to take advantage of every opportunity to state your goal and be specific about it. Otherwise, you do not know where you are going. If you want food, you cannot just say, "Oh, I want food." No, if you want to eat, you say, "I'm going to the grocery store." Or "I'm going to Chipotle today." Or "I'm going to go get a fresh organic quinoa meat power bowl to get my daily fiber in because I'm trying to fit into my green speedo with a black leprechaun on the front." You cannot just say "I'm hungry" and expect food to appear. This is where *I am, I can, I will* helps. These statements can help you overcome your obstacles in a focused manner.

During one of my first practices as a freshman at Notre Dame, I faced a challenge. For a week and a half, there was one particular player who literally beat the crap out of me on a daily basis. Every day in drills, he took me down. One time I was even knocked out of my cleat! One cleat on, one cleat God knows where, and I was sprawled out on the ground making noises I did not know I could make.

I could not beat him. I could not outsmart him. I was physically and mentally destroyed after each practice. Finally, I decided I had to do something. I had a choice: give up or change my mindset. That night, I said to myself, "I am Ryan Harris, I can turn this camp around by focusing on getting better one drill at a time. I can beat him in this one drill tomorrow. I will." I chose one specific drill in one specific opportunity that I knew would happen the next day and focused on it. I played it over and over in my head. I repeated *I can*. I was determined to beat my two-cleated foe. The next day, when that drill came up, I demolished and destroyed the guy who had been destroying me.

A week and a half before that moment, I had the opposite mindset. I went into those drills thinking, "I'm too small. I can't do it. I'm not as strong. I won't be able to play with these guys. These guys are going to kick my ass every day." And every day, that exact thing happened. But the moment I chose a mindset that built resolve, willingness, and action, everything changed. I had done the same drill against the same person for ten days in a row. It was not until my mindset changed that my performance improved. Even after beating that one guy on that one play, there were still times that he would beat me, but now I had a different mindset. I did not view a bad play as being beat up; I saw it as an opportunity, not a failure. It did not destroy my mentality or embarrass me. It was something I could learn from. *I am Ryan Harris, I can learn from that play, I will.*

Using *I am, I can, I will,* creates opportunities where you might not believe they exist. They inspire you immediately, no matter what you are facing. Try it now. I challenge you to say the words *I am, I can, I will* to whatever obstacle you are currently facing. After you say those phrases, do you still see them as an obstacle? Do you feel the resolve? Do you feel the beyond you just created?

Try applying the three phrases to other areas of your life as well. Career, relationships, hobbies. Think about these places and come up with a few phrases for yourself. Say them out loud. *I am. I can. I will.*

I am _____. I can have a great day today. I will.

I am _____. I can take it easy in this yoga class today. I will.

I am _____. I can nail this job interview. I will.

These phrases can even take you to places you had only dreamed. They create your beyond. Imagine if you started your day with, "I am _____. I can _____. I will _____. How could you not achieve something that day?

These phrases now belong to you. Use them when you wake in the morning. Use them at a board meeting. Use them to enter a difficult conversation with someone who does not make you happy. Use them to help you create the life you want.

That begins your mindset for mastery.

Zen culture has a saying: "Everything starts with a peaceful mind." Whether you are repairing a bike or making coffee, you must begin at peace. With the mindset of mastery, everything starts with a commitment to achieving your goal. If you have a mindset of committing to achieving your goals, you will experience no failure, only lessons. You will achieve your goals. Even the way you walk, stand, and speak will be full of your mindset, your belief in yourself, your future.

Having belief in yourself can be powerful. That belief becomes the rocket fuel behind your vision. Once you have belief, you will begin to visualize what you want before it happens. You will literally see your goals come to fruition.

CHAPTER TWO

VISUALIZE THE PRIZE

"Before the (Olympic) trials I was doing a lot of relaxing exercises and visualization. And I think that that helped me to get a feel of what it was gonna be like when I got there. I knew that I had done everything that I could to get ready for that meet, both physically and mentally."

—MICHAEL PHELPS

"Make sure you visualize what you really want, not what someone else wants for you."

—JERRY GILLIES

The next step to take in your mindset for mastery comes through visualization. You have just learned to strengthen the belief in yourself using *I am, I can, I will*, now you can visualize the prize. What big goal do you have right now? Do you want to retire young? Buy a house? Win that promotion? Find the love of your life? Ask yourself what that goal is, and then start to visualize it.

I always wrote down three goals before every game I played. Going into the playoffs Super Bowl 50 season, I did it again. Win after win, I declared my goals.

My goals would change from game to game, but I would always stick to three. For the Super Bowl, my goals were, "Overcome my fears and mistakes. Have fun and raise the trophy."

The night before the big game, I read them out loud and visualized them. When I got to my final goal—raise the trophy—I sat on my hotel bed, closed my eyes, and visualized what that looked like. When I visualized that moment, my family was there, and the loudest laughter and joy I had ever heard was all around me. My jersey had grass and paint stains from the field, and I was dripping sweat. I was excited. We had just won the Super Bowl. I could see myself as a champion. My teammates were all around me celebrating. Then it was all of us taking turns on holding the trophy. And for some reason, when I was holding the trophy, I could only see it from the bottom up. "That's weird," I thought. I had never touched the Lombardi Trophy, let alone known what it looked like from the bottom up. Yet that was what I kept seeing when I visualized the moment. It was completely real.

Then, the craziest thing happened. Twenty-four hours later, Peyton Manning handed me the trophy from the stage above. There it was. The first time I had ever touched the Lombardi trophy, the first time I had seen any trophy I had received in seventeen years of playing football, I saw it from the bottom up.

VISUALIZATION BECOMES REALITY

There is science that says when you visualize your success, your brain thinks it is real. World champion performance psychologist Dr. Rick Perea presents the science behind seeing our success, noting, "...through positive imagery, visualization, the brain will generate new pathways and prune away negative pathways." Think about that. You can literally remove negative thoughts and expectations by visualizing the positive! The first time I touched the Lombardi trophy, I felt I had been there before. And I remember thinking, "How the heck does that happen?"

Visualizing your goals gives you consciousness.

Ever wondered why your favorite champion, leader, or role model can do an interview after their big moment without being completely flustered? It is not because it is part of their job; it is because they are not surprised. They all visualized what that success looked like, and it did not catch them off guard.

Champions are not flustered by the fact that they just made a game-winning shot to save the playoffs. Or the fact that their whole world is on fire, and their family is there, and their friends are seeing it, and they have got 750 text messages when they come back to the locker room congratulating them. Champions can remain calm and collected in their biggest triumphs because they have seen that moment happen. When suddenly there is a microphone in front of their face, they know what to say. They have visualized the questions and the answers.

If you do not visualize achieving your goals, you will not put in the work to make your vision a reality. However, if you see yourself in that moment, you will be willing to do anything to get there. If your goal is to retire at forty-five, what does that look like? Does that mean you have $2 million in the bank and your house is paid off? Does it mean you have freedom to spend more time with your family or travel? To truly visualize the prize, you have to know every detail of achieving it. What are the specifics? What did the journey look like getting there? Was it a struggle? Was there sacrifice? What were the small wins you celebrated every day? What were the big wins you celebrated along the way? Were your failures worth it? Was it worth it?

Picture every detail possible. That way, when you get where you are going, you have already been there. You do not become flustered. You get to experience more than happiness and joy. You get to experience recognition, too! To be familiar with the moment as a champion was the greatest feeling I ever experienced in sports. Knowing that my teammates and I had believed and visualized our success took us beyond winning, beyond sharing the trophy with each other and loved ones. Experiencing what I visualized changed my life forever.

SET YOUR GOALS FOR YOU

The greatest performers of all time know that most of their accomplishments will go unnoticed by others. Yours will too. People look at me now as financially stable. They see me as a champion, a broadcaster, or a real estate investor. But that was not always how they saw me. Back then, to them, I was just another football player trying to get by. To others, I was a chubby kid in glasses who did not know how to play football. Yet, often, I had one thing others did not. I had my mindset. I had visualized my success. I had belief in myself. I had the willingness that comes from *I am, I can, I will.* I had clearly defined goals. I did not set those goals for other people. I did not do all that work to impress others. I did it to find out whether I could perform to my own potential. If I did not want to be financially stable or a world champion, no one would have ever seen that in me.

You must see yourself in your success before other people see it in you. People might think you are crazy for shooting for the stars. So what? Write your goals down anyway. Put them into your day. Make them known. People might laugh. People might mock you. But do you want to retire at forty-five for them? Or do you want to do it for yourself?

When I was in college, I had a screensaver that said, "Twenty-two-year-old millionaire." At that time, I was eating macaroni twice a week. I was nowhere near being a millionaire. I was still in school. I was studying hard and playing football as hard as I could, but I had no money. That screensaver was a daily reminder of where I wanted to go. It was my way of visualizing the prize. My roommates laughed at me. Others thought I was crazy. But the goal was mine. I had seen it. Eventually, when I made it to the NFL, two of my closest buddies told me, "You did it. You're a twenty-two-year-old millionaire." But that was not the reason I set that goal.

I did not do it for them. I did not write it down for them. I wrote it down to remind myself. I spelled it out to put myself in that place of being a twenty-two-year-old millionaire when I was tired, when I did not want to do the work. I knew what taking advantage of my opportunity looked like, and because of that I had faith in the steps it took to get there. It did not matter what others thought. I was willing to do the work and hold myself accountable to my goal every day.

What does success look like to you?

For you to visualize your goals, they have to be clearly defined. Take a moment right now, or the next time you are free, and write down your goals. After you do that, put them in a place where you will see them daily. Maybe you write them down and put them by your bed. Maybe you set a calendar appointment to remind yourself of them daily. Maybe you put a note on your mirror in your bathroom. Whatever you do, do something that makes the most sense to you. Do not worry what others might think. Use *your* goals to keep *you* going.

VISUALIZATION KEEPS YOU GOING

Sometimes, just putting your goal out there is confidence enough to keep you going. Other times, you need a push. When I sat down at my computer with that screensaver, I would ask myself, "Did I do something today to take me toward that goal?" A successful mindset lies in that questioning. That is the thing people will not see. The constant reminder. The daily tasks that bring you closer to the goal.

Remember, when you have the right mindset, people will be wrong about you all the time. That is not your problem. It is theirs. Your confidence to state your goals will build coherence within yourself that becomes proof for other people.

Holding the Lombardi trophy was far more than just that photographic moment. There were big and small wins along the way. Setbacks too. Nine different surgeries, three of them on my back, getting released, moving, moving back, missing my son's first words because I was in St. Joseph, Missouri. Someone might have seen me grabbing that trophy, but nobody else saw what went into that achievement. Few people were around for the thousands of hours of training, watching film, and committing to improvement. In your life, no one will see how hard you worked for your success, the sacrifices you made, or the ways you reinforced your dreams. Embrace this aspect of your mastery. Work hard. And go beyond setting goals by visualizing them.

VISUALIZE YOUR WAY THROUGH THE FEAR

Visualization can also be a great way to work out your fears and anxieties regarding an upcoming event. When you visualize, you are able to recognize triggers specific to you, and you can work through them without the pressure of the actual moment.

We talk about fear less than we talk about sex, yet it is a huge component of everything we do in life. Want to know a truth about sports? Everyone experiences fear. Want to know a truth about life? Everyone experiences fear. While we do not talk about fear, we also do not talk about how to work through it. Visualization can be a powerful tool for you and your performance, which allows you to recognize your fears and go beyond them.

You may call it being anxious or upset. You may call it being an introvert, but there are fears going on in all of us.

Visualization is a great way to recognize your fear and work through it. To seek mastery includes understanding how fear manifests itself in your life. I had teammates that would play loud music, talk to their parents, talk to their girlfriends, walk around the field barefoot before a game, or even vomit to handle their fear. Every masterful performance you have ever seen has been done *with* fear. That's right, *with* fear. Mastering yourself includes knowing how to move forward beyond your fear. You are going to have fear one way or another, so why not perform with that fear instead of letting it stop you?

When you are visualizing playing in your championship game, think about what might distract you from your goal. Think about how fear might manifest itself. Then plan for it. I understood what fear looked like for me before games. It was constant nagging thoughts of doubt, so I told myself, "Negative thoughts don't matter." Even if I am visualizing going to the locker room and then I worry, "What if we lose this game?" I am able to work through it. What matters is that I am walking through this locker room. I am going to put on my pads. I am going to get ready for the game. I might become nervous. I might worry about losing. I can smile at these thoughts because I will play a great game. Because I have visualized the important things, I realize fear does not matter. Now I can move with the fear.

When we focus on fear, we limit our possibilities. When

I would feel self-doubt, I came to understand it was a natural part of high performance. I embraced my fears through visualization and did not let them stop me from seeing success. I would say, "Okay, there's my fear. I must be on the way to achieving something great." Fear can become a distraction that takes you away from your goals. You will always have thoughts of failure and doubt. Find understanding in them and allow those very same thoughts to give you confidence that you are achieving your greatness.

Negative thoughts are just that, thoughts. They are not real. But if you give them too much space in your head, then they will become real. If you think you are not ready, you are too tired, or you have concerns, those things will all happen. If you think, "I am ready. I am going to have a great day. I am going to win," then you can achieve everything you pictured. You can hold up the trophy of your goals and have that moment where everything you visualized becomes reality.

CHAPTER THREE

Pick Up a Shovel and Dig

"There's always one more thing you can do."

—COL. HAL MOORE

At this point in working toward the mindset of mastery, you have done all the prep work. You believe in yourself and now visualize your goals. You have written down your goals, and you know you can accomplish them.

Now comes the real work.

If you want to accomplish greatness, you must to be willing to roll up your sleeves and get dirty. Do yourself a favor and pick up a shovel and dig. You have to take the tools found in belief and visualization and slam them into action.

Every building you have ever been into started as a pile of dirt. Someone came along and placed a shovel in the earth with the belief and visualization of creating a great building. Your mindset, your goals, will come in the very same way. If you want to accomplish your dreams, you have to actually do the work. You have to put a shovel in the dirt and start digging.

There are over 200 diamonds in the Super Bowl 50 ring. How many do you think were lying on the ground waiting to be picked up? None.

How many diamonds in your life are just lying around, waiting to be picked up?

I find it amazing how many people will believe in themselves and visualize their success but choose not to do any work toward it. I meet people every day who have immense reservoirs of talent, willpower, and resolve but are unwilling to work.

People can get lazy. They think, "I have talent. I can do this," and they do not want to put in the extra effort. They think they have it all figured out and they do not have to keep working. But if you want that new job, then you have to put in all the work to get it. You have to go beyond the work you think it will take.

The greatest teammates I ever had did not do the bare minimum. Barack Obama failed in his first political run, but he kept going. Apple started with the Marquis computer, but the company did not stop there; it went beyond. Your favorite friends and leaders go beyond the bare minimum. As a parent, you do more than just donate your sperm and eggs. You culture, you nurture, you provide. If you were in a relationship and your partner only did the bare minimum of things you asked, chances are you probably would not be happy in that relationship. You do not just get a dog and feed it. You take it for walks and play with it. You take way too many photos and post them on social media.

Everything that has value in life requires you to go beyond.

Your digging will always take tough work. You might literally have to go into an uncomfortable, dark place to reach the other side. Legendary geologist Jim Howe once told me that often his job was to go into mines with a headlamp, a shovel, and some tools. At six-feet-five-inches, he had to work in a space that was five-and-a-half feet tall and fifteen feet wide. Sometimes, he would have to use the headlamp to dig and make space to walk, because his hands could not move in the dirt. How uncomfortable do you think he was?

There will be times where you get knocked down, when

you feel like it is too hard to keep going; just keep putting the shovel in the dirt. You cannot build a hospital to save lives unless you are willing to dig the foundation. You cannot become a champion unless you are willing to practice.

WHEN YOUR GOOD IS NOT GOOD ENOUGH

When your good is not good enough, pick up a shovel and dig. Deny yourself failure; dig into the work. Dig into making yourself better. Dig into creating a path for success.

Often, that means trying new things!

Before our Super Bowl season, I knew I had to find a way to recover faster physically. With this particular future Hall of Famer, we ran plays every fifteen seconds compared to every thirty seconds. Hey, that's an eternity for a three-hundred-pounder! If I was out of breath, I was behind. My hard breathing and mental triggers were holding me back. I had to be able to hear a play and perform while gasping for air. This was new for me. So, I decided to seek out renowned MMA coach Marc Montoya and trainer Wade Brinkman to re-learn how to breathe. That is right, in my ninth year in the NFL, I had to learn how to breathe! And it did wonders!

That is just one of the many times when my good was not

good enough. What are you willing to do? If you want a new job, maybe you need to revise your resume. Search for the right opening, network with new people, and try new things. You might have to take a class to improve your skills. You might need to find a mentor. Whatever it is, are you willing to take those steps to get ahead? You cannot simply say, "I hate my job. I need a new one," and expect results. You need to figure out the exact steps you need to take to get there and start digging.

Once you start digging, you are creating. You are creating a way out, a way in, a way up.

The Empire State Building is an amazing building. You might have stood on the streets of New York City and looked up at it in awe, but have you ever stopped to think about how that building came into existence? How many shovels had to dig its foundation? How many people had to learn a skill to build it? How many hours did it take before it was 102 stories high? How many people had to persevere before it became an iconic sight?

I bet there were plenty of times when people wanted to give up, but they did not. They did the work, and they were glad they did. You might not be building a literal skyscraper, but that does not mean there is less digging to be done. When you are not where you want to be, pick up a shovel and dig. Persevere through the difficult times.

Seventy percent of people I know quit as soon as it is up to them to find a solution. It takes a mindset of mastery that is willing to put the shovel in the dirt and work after a setback or a loss.

WORK THROUGH THE PAIN

Too often, people get to this point where things are really tough, and they do not want to go forward. "It's too hard," they say. "I'm not good enough." The truth is no matter how hard it gets, you are going to live beyond those moments. You are going to get past the embarrassment, the pain, and the failure. So if you are going to live beyond those tough moments, why not choose how you are going to get there?

I was on an NFL team that lost fourteen games in a row. Fourteen! I had my car and apartment shipped home before the last game because I could not wait to get home and put the season behind me. More than that, I wanted to work the stink of loss off me as soon as possible, and that meant there was digging to be done. I was not the only one to think this way. My teammates and coaches did too. Instead of accepting defeat, we said, "This is not the end of our story. We're going to continue along this path." We worked through the losing season, practiced harder in the off-season, and came back the next year stronger than ever. Those very same coaches and many of those same players from that losing team went on to win Super Bowl 50 after getting fired for poor performance.

We picked up the shovel and dug to become champions.

Where can you put the shovel in and start digging? If you are in that dead-end job and you want to make a change, what steps are you taking to realize your dream?

Maybe you have already been digging, but the market is tough. Maybe you have been on ten interviews, but you cannot seem to land an offer. If you are figuratively on your knees, embarrassed, put the shovel back in the dirt and use it to help you stand up again. When your good is not good enough, do the work.

If you want a new job, do not look at the rejections as failure. Look at them as a chance to learn. What are you missing? What can you do right now to be a more attractive candidate? What can you strengthen? What can you do to be better? What industry have you not tried? What can you start with today?

THE DAILY DIG

There exists a phrase *dig a hole, make it wide,* meaning "as you work, build yourself options." You might need to adjust your plans. You might need to turn left instead of right. The important thing is that you keep moving. Keep digging. If the rewritten resume does not land you an interview, write it again. Or create something new to draw attention to your experience and expertise. Maybe that means posting an article on LinkedIn or taking an improv comedy class. If your connections do not pay off, meet new people. Keep making movements toward your goal. When your good is not good enough, put two hands on the shovel and lift. Slug it through the dirt. Be willing to get dirty, sweaty, and knocked down. The work you do will separate you from everyone else around you. That work creates the power of your mindset that will lead to your success. That is the work you have to do every day.

Too many people fail to practice what they depend on every day for success.

Every day in the NFL I would practice footwork, timing, and movements—the essentials of becoming a great lineman. Most times I would be the only one doing these drills before practice. Amazingly, even younger players who were not playing did not work on their crafts at all. I thought that was crazy. Why are these young cats, who are not playing, not working on some of the things that are going to make them successful? They have this extra opportunity, yet they are wasting it.

This happens in every business.

If footwork is part of your success, practice it every day. If asking questions is part of your success, practice it every day. Figure out the basic fundamentals that you can always work on. Then do them every day, even the parts that you hate. As a rookie in the NFL, they made me make coffee every day, and I hated it. For one thing, I did not know how to make coffee. For another, no matter what mood I was in or how much time I had, I had one more thing to do: coffee. At the time, I thought these guys just loved giving me a task out of pure laziness. I know now that they were teaching me the habit of doing something every day, even the things I hated.

What is that daily task you hate but know will pay off in the end? Do that. If you have to show up earlier than you want to in order to be ready for a meeting or to answer those emails, do it. If you want to build relationships, but you do not like networking, take a risk and talk to someone new. Call the person you do not have to. Say yes to an invitation that scares the crap out of you. Do the things that are difficult. Do the things you do not like, because those are the action pieces you need. Those are what help you move forward toward your goal.

When you set a routine, you also create for yourself the opportunity to be consistent with your actions. Repetition, routine, and rhythm are part of success. Create a mindset and willingness to work hard. Bruce Lee once said, "I fear not the man who practiced 10,000 kicks once, but I fear the man who has practiced one kick 10,000 times."

To create the first Dyson vacuum, the company made over 700 prototypes. That's 700 times they built a vacuum that did not work. Now Dyson stands as the top vacuum sold in every American household. I bet James Dyson is glad he kept digging. He persevered. He was willing to pick up his shovel and dig to achieve his goal. And deep down, you are that willing too.

PRACTICE ACCOMPLISHMENT

Going through what you do not like makes you better at what you do like. When you spend your time doing something you hate, you appreciate the things you love. Additionally, every time you do something that you do not like doing, you are practicing accomplishment.

Much success comes from these very things we hate. For example, I hate running. I hate it so much that I have run in jeans before because I knew if I took the time to change, I would make an excuse not to run. Yet running was a huge part of my job in the NFL. If I did not practice running, I would not have made it. Even though I hated it, I still ran. I still put my shovel in the dirt and dug. I ran in my jeans because that was the work I had to do. I knew that running was the best thing for me. It created speed and agility. Even though I hated it, it was good for me.

As a rookie, when I spent time in the facility, I could not stand it. I used to say, "I want to go home. I want to do the work at home." But when I became a veteran and stayed to study more film and worked on my core to support my back, I found greater enjoyment when I *was* home, because I was present. Anytime you can create appreciation in your life, you are building a mindset that will help you achieve. After every run, I felt accomplished. I was literally farther from the person I was when I was sitting on the couch making excuses.

People often say, "I just don't like doing that," or "I don't like that aspect of the job." They like the fun parts, but they do not like the hard parts. When I talk to schools or youth programs, even at colleges, kids tell me school is not their thing. They just want to play ball. I remind them that school makes you a better football player. You have to go to college for three years if you want to make it to the NFL. Plus, in the NFL, you have to be in a classroom for four or five hours a day. I tell the kids who want to be athletes that if they do not like taking notes or sitting in a classroom, they will not be on the field with me or any other professional football player. We will not allow it. They have to put in the work in the classroom if they ever want to put on their pads in the pros.

We had a Hall-of-Fame and world-champion coach remind us daily that "Everyone has something shitty about their job; embrace it." Embrace the things you do not like so you can experience the things you do like. No one likes waking up early to go to school or work. No one likes confrontation. No one likes studying for a difficult test. I did not like practicing ten hours a day. I did not like waking up in pain after a Sunday game. But I did it, and I am glad I did because it allowed me to achieve my goals.

GO ANYWHERE FOR A DIAMOND

When I was between teams in the middle of my career, I got a call from the Kansas City Chiefs. They wanted me to try out with them before they signed me. The call came in at 1:00 p.m., and I was booked for a flight at 3:30 p.m. for a workout at 8:00 a.m. the next morning. I did not know if I would be signed to that team, but I took the risk. I saw the opportunity and went for it. I packed a small bag with enough clothes for the practice the next morning and hopped on the plane. After the 8:00 a.m. workout, the team said they wanted to sign me. They had the paperwork ready, and there was a conditioning test at 3:00 p.m. I said, "I'm happy to do it, but you've got to take me to Walmart to get some underwear." I made a plan to do the work. After the 10:00 a.m. meeting, I went to Walmart at 11:00 a.m. to buy underwear, white T-shirts, and a pair of sweatpants for a run at 3:00 p.m. I never thought I would find myself alone in the underwear aisle in St. Joseph, Missouri, preparing for success, but that is where my shovel took me.

Being willing to leave my house without enough clothes changed my life drastically in just two days. Sometimes, you might be sweaty, joked on by millionaires for your St. Joseph, Missouri Walmart clothes and flip flops. It will be okay; you will live. You might be going to a movie by yourself because you do not have friends in the place you are moving. You might not know a single person outside of your job. That is okay. Use that headlamp. Pick up a shovel and dig. Keep going. Keep creating your beyond. Enjoy the journey.

NO EXCUSES

A vision remains worthless without action. *I am, I can, I will* is a great thing to say. But if you do not take action, it remains empty. Throughout my life, I have seen people around me who were not able to achieve, because they made excuses. At Notre Dame, there was so much potential wasted. There were players who could have gone on to the pros but were not willing to do the work. Friends and colleagues were unwilling to sacrifice in order to make the most of an opportunity. Throughout my entire ten-year NFL career, I watched people fail to do the work. It was tragic. I once knew a kid who had played at a premiere Division I football program and made it to the NFL. He had the talent to succeed, but there was one problem. His weight. It was too high to continue playing in the NFL. He ignored our coach and thought he could get by on talent alone. He would not do the hard work to get his weight under control. He still thought he would play in the NFL. He did not. He was fired.

Think about this. At the time of publication, the current commissioner of the NFL, Roger Goodell, signed a $45-million-a-year contract with access to a private jet. His first job in the NFL? He started as the driver for Pete Rozelle, the now-former NFL commissioner. Do you think Roger liked being a driver? Fifteen years later, do you think he likes being an NFL commissioner? At $45 million a year now, I bet he is happy he took a job as a driver and navigated his way to the top. He understood the days and years you have to put in to achieve what you want to achieve. What a mindset.

ACKNOWLEDGE THE SMALL STUFF

Part of picking up a shovel is acknowledging small improvements. Appreciate every single small improvement that you see and feel. Maybe you did not land the new job, but the interviewer was impressed by your revised resume. Acknowledge that. Maybe you were one of two remaining candidates. Appreciate that you have come this far. No one else is going to recognize that for you. Be your own cheerleader.

Part of being your own cheerleader includes forgiveness.

Forgive yourself for your failures. Improve and learn from your mistakes. Forgive yourself for not winning the job. Forgive yourself for not being the best parent at that time, at that moment. Forgive yourself for missing that call from your loved one. Mistakes will be made, but you have a shovel to dig your way out of it. Pick up your shovel and dig.

When you create this space for yourself, you begin to reap the many benefits of forgiveness. One of the most unsuspected benefits will be accountability. By forgiving yourself, you recognize where you fell and where you need to work harder. When your mentality is to dig when you fall, you are going to keep working. You can move past that point when your good is not good enough. You have a choice. You decide if you are willing to live your wildest dreams. You decide if you are willing to persevere.

CHAPTER FOUR

PERSEVERE

"It's not whether you get knocked down, it's whether you get up."

—VINCE LOMBARDI

"Determine that today you will overcome your self of the day before, tomorrow you will win over those of lesser skill, and later you will win over those of greater skill."

—MIYAMOTO MUSASHI

Now that you have your beliefs, visualization, and willingness to keep digging, you will undoubtedly be tested. You will get knocked down. No matter what form this takes in your journey, stay the course and persevere. At some point, you are going to think reaching your goal is way too much work. Whether you are meeting someone new or starting a new job, you may think, "I don't know how

I'll be able to accomplish it all." Despite all the obstacles you will face, you have to keep going. You have to keep digging. You have to stay the course.

On the way to achieving your greatness, you are going to hurt. You are going to lose friends. You are going to make enemies. You are going to be a different person on the other side of it. Perseverance comes through how you handle your failures. How much are you willing to endure in order to succeed? How embarrassed are you willing to get if that embarrassment creates the perspective and skills that get you to where you are supposed to be?

Remember, **you have a choice in how you respond to failure.** Most people will not risk success, because they fear embarrassment. If you have ever hiked a mountain, you know the last quarter mile is tougher than the first three miles. It is a higher elevation and a higher incline. Yet to get to the top, you put one foot in front of the other. The same is true in life.

When I met my wife, I was willing to go up and talk to her, to ask if we could meet sometime, to ask her out to dinner. Even if she'd said, "Sorry, I've got a boyfriend," or "No, that's okay," I am glad I took that risk. I am glad I did not walk away. I think my kids are too.

PERSEVERANCE LEADS TO SUCCESS

Two months into my first year in the NFL, I needed to have another surgery. I had just recovered from my first ever surgery and done the rehab to get drafted into the NFL. I was feeling strong and ready. I was putting in the work and time to be a champion. Then, boom. I had to have my second back surgery. I refused to let that stop me. I stayed the course to becoming a champion. I had the surgery and went to physical therapy. I dug deep and did the work that put me back on the field. I was the only black guy in yoga and Pilates class for years. I was the only three-hundred-pound man in the pool, rehabbing my back, swimming to regain my health. I got back in the game.

Then, after a successful year where I was three games away from a million-dollar bonus, I dislocated my toe. I was again out of the game. My mountain got steeper and harder to climb. I was literally climbing my stairs on my knees because I could not walk, but I continued to stay the course. I came back from the toe injury and made it back onto the field. I played as hard as I could.

Then I got benched. I pushed harder in practice. I trained harder in the gym. I got named a starter again. "Finally," I thought, "I got off the bench for good." Then I got released. The mountain became slippery. The air up top was thin. But I kept going. I got signed to another team.

Then I had to have my third back surgery. After that, I was released again. I was en route back to the airport hotel in Philadelphia when my agent called to tell me I was being let go. When I arrived in the dark hotel room that evening, I was destroyed—unwanted, unhealthy, and thousands of miles from home. The despair was stronger than it had ever been. I was grasping at that moment for anything to do.

In that moment, I said, "I *can* pray. I can pray the most difficult prayer of my life. I can be grateful for the career I had." After that prayer, I looked for more. I kept climbing the mountain. "I *can* call Dr. Josh Sandell to see how I can recover fast. I *can* call my trainer, Ted Johnson, to tell him we are going to work for a comeback." The words I *can* truly lifted me out of a dark hotel room into a future of what I could do. I rehabbed, went back to practice, and eventually made it back to the Broncos. I got released again, went to the Texans and the Chiefs, and then returned to the Broncos for a magical Super Bowl-winning season.

I then went on to Pittsburgh, where I almost lost my lower leg and had five surgeries to keep it. All throughout my career, I fought self-doubt, physical and mental pain, and embarrassment. Hell, I even fought my teammates at times. The one thing that gave me ability in all those moments was my shovel. I kept working. I kept going. I persevered.

I even faced failures in school. Anyone else? Bueller?

When I was in college, I really loved studying economics. When I got a D-minus on the first test, I did not jump out of the class and change my major. I did more. I went to teaching hours. I got a tutor. I dug deeper and stayed the course because I believed in myself. Three and a half years later, I graduated with a degree in economics and policy.

When I first put on my pads and did not know how to hit, I could have quit right there. I could have said, "People don't like me. I'm in a new place. I don't know what I'm doing, and this isn't for me."

I failed for eight seasons in the NFL before I became a Super Bowl champion. Even in that ninth season, there were failures along the way. We did not win every game. I had to overcome a knee injury in addition to the wear and tear of a twenty-four-week NFL season to win the Super Bowl. Throughout my career, I missed games. Things hurt, physically and mentally. But I stayed the course.

I know I am not alone here. My failures are not unique. Your failures are not unique. That is the common thread in every success story. Our willingness to fail.

So many people have said to me, "I want to play in the

NFL." My response is always, "Great, are you willing to make a mistake in front of 70,000 people in a stadium? Are you willing to get yelled at in front of sixty-five people in a room? Are you willing to have your best friends bring up your worst moments because those were funny to them?" That's playing in the NFL. Being willing to fail in front of thousands of people is playing pro football. Are you willing to do that?

Perseverance means working your way through the failure and reframing it. If you look at the failures you have had in your life, how many of them have you overcome? I am willing to bet that it would be just about all of them. If you have not overcome a failure, you have learned from it. What a powerful tool.

LeBron James knows this about failure as well. "You have to be able to accept failure to get better," he once said.

How are you at accepting failure? How are you at persevering through failure?

You will face setbacks. Failures. Mistakes. You might not be able to afford the car you wanted to buy. Your job title might not bring enough clout for you. You might not be providing for your family in the way you want to. You might not get that bonus or impress your boss. No matter what happens, **you have a choice** in how you handle these setbacks. **Your mindset when failure occurs will dictate your success.** Your failures are the greatest teaching tool you can find. Use them to your advantage.

When you have your mindset for mastery, what someone may perceive as a failure will not be a failure for you. Someone might identify failure as not getting into the school you want. But maybe by not getting into that big school, you have a chance to attend a smaller institution that provides you a more tailored education. Maybe it sets you on a path to a future career you had never considered. Or to a love you would have never met. Use your failures as opportunities to move and to grow.

In the darkest times of your journey, remember that you already persevered to reach that point. Believe in your experience, and create the other side that you have not reached yet. When you persevere, you can invest your time and energy in the right places, things, and people. That's living life.

ELIMINATE DISTRACTIONS

Along your way, you may need to give your perseverance a boost. One of the best ways I have found to do this comes from learning how to recognize distractions. When you make it to new places and are doing new things, even when you are on the road to achieving what you want to achieve, you rarely think about the distractions. If you want to strengthen your perseverance, identify your distractions. What are they? Think about the who, what, when, and why of your life when it comes to distractions.

Who is a distraction in your life?

What can you identify as a distraction in your life? TV? Phone? Game night?

Why are certain people, places, and things distractions in your life?

I love going to Vegas, for example. The city has fantastic food and great entertainment, but sometimes I do not need to be going to Vegas. Sometimes I need to be working on a speech or a broadcast segment. When I was playing football, sometimes I needed to be practicing footwork instead of checking my phone for texts or looking at social media. Sometimes I would not even turn on the TV when we arrived at the team hotel, to get focused. When you start to examine your distractions, you can see the areas in your life where you can improve. Recognizing your distractions can also serve as a wake-up call. Sometimes you need to fire someone. Sometimes you need to quit your job. You might need to break up with someone, find a new teacher, or learn a new skill. The difference between having resolve in life and resigning yourself to your circumstances comes by moving past your failures and distractions. Have the courage to face difficulties and move through them. Be honest with yourself. Face your realities. Find your distractions and take action.

Sometimes even those you love most can be a distraction. Think about how you can readjust those relationships to eliminate the distractions in a given time. Those who love you and care about you will be part of your success. They will never stand in the way of what you want to accomplish. They will always understand what you see as distractions. For me, people used to come in on a Friday night of a home game and stay until Sunday, but Friday night in the NFL was my Wednesday. I would not show up at their jobs and expect them to take me out and have fun when they had to work for two more days. To eliminate the distraction, I started telling people to come on Saturday afternoon and stay until Monday. That immediately weeded out a variety of visitors and distractions.

It will also be important for your mindset to ask yourself why certain things are a distraction. Often, distractions point to something deeper. Why is this person I am in a relationship with distracting me from what I want to be doing? It might not be the person you need to be with. Why am I not applying for a job that I really want but might be underqualified for? You might fear failure and the ability to succeed. Why do I keep looking for new job postings? You might be in a job you do not want to be in.

When you examine your distractions, it forces you to ask yourself whether you really believe in your dreams enough to do the work. Distractions are also a way of telling you that you are ignoring the hard work that needs to be done.

My teammates who were not willing to do the work had so many distractions. They could not stay for practice because of this or that. They had to leave meetings early for golf. Sometimes they would skip the shower so they could make their tee time. They could not save money because they needed to buy their happiness. They could not watch film because...You probably know these people, too. Great teams, great leaders, and even your greatness understand the distraction these people bring.

Successful teams acknowledge distractions.

When we made it to the Super Bowl, we had a meeting where the coaches and staff laid out all the distractions. Coach said, "Hey, I know you all have family coming to town. That's great, but remember we're here on a mission. Remember, you've still got a job to do. You didn't win the Super Bowl yet."

Acknowledging these distractions is what great teams do. They also endear you to your leader and your teammates because you do not feel like you are the only one excited about showing your family the perks of being at that game. It allows you to feel excited but also remember that you are there to accomplish something. That acknowledgment emboldens and empowers people to feel their feelings but also gives the opportunity to focus.

There will always be failures and distractions no matter what part of the journey you are in. What can you do to eliminate those distractions? If you need to sleep more, but you are watching TV, ask yourself, "Is the TV helping me?" If turning off the TV helps you pick up a book or get better sleep, what are you doing watching TV? Or TV might be a distraction during the week but rewarding on the weekend. Sometimes you want a distraction. Putting in the work and winning the Super Bowl made me want to go to a beach somewhere. You need to create time for yourself. But did I need to be on a beach just before or during the season? No.

Put in the work. Eliminate your distractions. Persevere.

When you persevere, you will move at a higher level and pace toward your dreams. You will invest your time in the right ways and be pulled toward your greatness.

CHAPTER FIVE

MASTER YOUR TIME

"No time for losers, 'cause we are the champions."

—QUEEN

You are well on your way to a mindset of mastery. You have gained the belief in yourself. You have visualized your success. You have dug in and persevered. Now comes the bridge to everywhere. When you invest your time in the people and things that reinforce the work you are doing, then you are mastering your time.

We have all heard the song "We Are the Champions" by Queen. I must have heard it a thousand times before we won the Super Bowl and a million times since. It was not until after we won the Super Bowl that I heard and recognized one of the most powerful verses of that song, "No time for losers 'cause we are the champions...of the world." I am not sure what it was; it could have been the transformation from pro athlete to forever champion, but for the first time, I understood those words *no time for losers.*

You see, when you have a mindset for mastery, you begin to realize, and others do too, that you operate on a different wavelength. Part of that for me meant saying no to partying and outings far more than I said yes. Another part was surrounding myself with people who contributed to my mindset. People who also had belief in themselves and their goals. People who wanted to achieve their greatness.

I want you to remember this one thing everywhere the path to your greatness takes you.

Not everyone is worth your time.

Again.

Not everyone is worth your time.

NO TIME FOR LOSERS

When you are on the path of your dreams, you have no time for losers. Losers are the people who distract you from your goals, talk you out of a workout, or wait for you to come back from busting your ass only to ask you to solve a problem they could not solve themselves while sitting on the couch.

Losers complain about their lives without taking action. They weaken your belief in yourself and waste your time when you could be digging. I have been amazed throughout my years in the NFL and now in retirement at how many people have losers around them!

How many people do you think asked for tickets to Super Bowl 50? How many of those same people do you think were there with me throughout my back surgeries and toe surgery? How many do you think called me after getting released by the Broncos, trained with me in the dark gyms of doubt and unemployment? How many people trained with me at Performance Athletics, Landow Performance, and more when I was digging for my goal? Not many.

I have had to separate myself from friends in high school, college, and my adult life because they like to complain, love to point out the wrong ways I do things, and hate to pick up a shovel and dig. I have no time to give these people. Neither do you. When you are achieving your greatness, you have no time for people who want you to bring them along.

You do not have a place in your mindset for people who

are not worth your time. You will never regret leaving those who are not worth your time, either. Embrace the freedom that comes from letting those people go, because it will give you more time to invest in the things that make you happy and help you achieve.

When you are working for what you want, tell those around you what you need.

Pay close attention to the people who surround you, because there are times when the great, loving people in your life have moments of being losers. They distract you from what you are trying to achieve. You might have friends, family, teammates, or coworkers who are supportive for most of the time, but then they have their moments when they want to distract you from the task at hand. They say, "Stay for one more drink," or, "Do you really have to go to work? Can't you hang with the family?" These are the people you need to lovingly tell that you have to focus on you.

In the NFL preseason training camp, I would tell my closest friends, "Expect to not hear from me for the next month and a half. I'll call you if I have time. I'm going dark outside of my day-to-day battle. You might think it's selfish, but I don't care. I'm trying to win a championship, and this is what I've got to do."

I kept this mindset during the NFL season. I locked into

work. I focused on my job. There were guys on my same team throughout the years who I would not spend time with because they were not digging in and putting in the work. There were teammates who I would not go out with because they wanted to celebrate at the club every night. I would not spend time going out to a party on a weekday before a game. In my eyes, there would be plenty of time to party after we won a Super Bowl. It may shock you to read that those teammates never won a Super Bowl. I invested my time in focusing on the goal. You have to take control of your time and invest it smartly.

Ask yourself, "Am I investing my time, or am I losing my time?" When you realize you are losing time with a place or a person, do not feel bad about it. Decide what you need to do to change the pattern, and do it. You have no time for losers. If they are contributing to your life, they will stay in your life. Do not feel bad that someone is making you lose your time. Pick up your shovel and dig away from them.

Right now, you are probably already thinking of a few people you probably should not hang out with. You have known it, but you have not done anything about it. You do not want to hurt their feelings or make things awkward. Forget that. You are on your way to your goals. They do not feel bad about wasting your time, so do not feel bad about moving on.

This is your path. Your journey. You have the choice to invest your time intelligently. If you do not take care of your time, no one will take care of it for you. Having a mindset for mastery means putting power behind your time.

VALUE AND INVEST YOUR TIME

Begin to place in your mindset where you can make decisions to *value your time*. Think about where you can take time from the distractions and put it toward reaching your goal.

Ask yourself, "Am I using my time to improve what I love and what I want to accomplish? Or am I using my time to distract myself from the hard work?" I used to hate getting to work early. I used to hate staying late. But when I made it to work earlier, I got my workout in earlier. I ate a better breakfast. When I stayed later, I learned more about my opponent. That one extra minute, where I watched one more play, meant that I could outsmart my opponent in that next game.

Saving and investing your time can look different for everyone. You might give yourself an extra fifteen minutes to get to a meeting, or cut a meeting fifteen minutes short. I met with an accomplished entrepreneur once who understood the value of time. In his nine-o'clock morning meetings, no one was allowed to sit. He believed if everyone was standing, no one would talk for too long. This cut the meetings down to the necessities. People were more engaged, and they saved time. They became productive.

Ask yourself where you can invest time now that will get you to your goals. If your goal is to buy a house, can you take on extra work hours to bolster your savings? If your goal is to run a marathon, can you skip Friday night happy hour to fit in another run? If you want to travel the world, can you skip a short weekend trip to save your paid time off? Where can you save time now that will give you freedom later?

With time, little moments add up. Spending five minutes here or an hour there browsing social media or playing video games seems fine until you find that you are nowhere near ready for that marathon you planned to run or the goal you said was so important to you. Now is the time to plan ahead. Not tomorrow. You might think you can train later for that twenty-six-mile race. But suddenly race day will be a few weeks away, and you will not be ready. If you had just run a small bit every day, you would be prepared for your goal.

Start small. You do not have to make drastic changes, but you have to be aware of where you are spending your time. Can you go to bed thirty minutes earlier to be more energized in the morning? Can you get to the office fifteen minutes earlier? Can you stay later at the office to pick up overtime? Can you wake up earlier to fit in a run before work? Can you skip work drinks to spend time with your family?

A smart time investment leads to greater opportunity for success. Hanging out with people who do not make you happy at happy hour affects every goal you have set for yourself.

FIND A MENTOR

One of the best ways to invest your time comes through spending time with mentors. No matter what industry you are in, someone has been there before. I must have played with one hundred rookies on the offensive line alone, and I can only remember two who asked for advice. That's crazy. The greatest gains in learning come through asking questions. Asking questions shows that you are engaged. When you ask questions, it also shows others that you want to contribute to a goal with efficiency.

Find a friend or family member who has had success and failures. Ask their advice for anything you are dealing with. Be honest with yourself about where you are, and be honest in the questions you ask. Do not dance around an issue. Instead say, "Hey, I'm really struggling right now with getting through my week, but I know this work needs to be done. How do you make sure to get all your work done?"

People in your field will answer your questions when they see you investing your time in the right things. They will give you their time for free. When you ask questions, you demonstrate a level of knowledge, belief, and commitment that most people do not have. Others will be happy to share what they have learned with you.

I have yet to find a mentor who has told me, "Ryan, I don't want to talk to you. I don't have time for you." Whatever you are learning, wherever you are in your journey, ask questions to people who have been where you want to go. Aaron Taylor, a Super Bowl champion and a mentor of mine, has done this numerous times for me. I have asked him questions on everything from footwork to how to approach ticket situations for friends and family to retirement. Because I showed interest and willingness to learn, he was willing to help me out.

Find a couple of mentors who have a similar or even a completely different viewpoint as you. Find someone who has accomplished something you can ask questions about. One of my mentors works in tech but is also a father. We talk about parenthood and stocks. Another of my mentors, the great Michael B. Daugherty, is a lawyer, and our conversations have saved me and my family money and headache.

A mentor can also give you the gift of helping you know where to invest your time. There's no use in working hard if you are working hard at the wrong thing. Mentors can help you invest your time in the place that matters most. Every successful person I know will go out of their way to give a mentee direction and efficiency. How can you know what pitfalls to avoid if you do not have a mentor in your field?

My first weeks in the NFL, I did not know how to read the playbook. They had so many defenses on the page that I could not decipher what was happening. I asked a veteran, "Hey, what's going on in this protection?" His response saved me time. He said, "We never run that play. If we do, it goes against this one defense. Don't waste your time beating it into your head."

"Thank you!" I said.

Had I not asked for help, I would have spent the evening trying to learn a play that did not matter. By asking for help, I then had more time to dedicate to the rest of the book.

What plays are you running that do not matter? What has

your mind all bent up, preventing you from producing? Don't ask me! Ask your mentor!

When you ask your mentor questions, it shows you are ready to do the work. Anybody in your field who is worth their weight will answer your questions and give you guidance. Look for opportunities to surround yourself with people who are willing to do the work. Sometimes they are hard to notice because they are finishing a task, doing something no one asked them to do, or arriving early. That is your new buddy. That is the person who can show you what working hard looks like in your field.

Investing your time with a mentor can bring huge dividends to your life. You are never wasting your time when you are with people who are achievers. You just might end up getting your kid into the right reading class, or sitting in on a meeting with a banker, or in the office of a coach who will take you to the Super Bowl.

SERVE

When I was a teenager, I used to wake up at 7:00 a.m. to serve breakfast with my school once a month at the Dorothy Day Center in St. Paul. During this time, I never looked forward to getting up that early and did so with the "want" to serve with the "willingness" of a teenage punk. One morning, I was stuck in my teenage morning fatigue when a woman leaned over the counter and loudly told me, "SMILE." I looked back at her and felt so embarrassed. Here was a woman who had only the clothes on her back. And there I was. I had slept in a warm bed. I had had access to a car to drive myself there. I was going to get a donut afterward. And I could not smile, but she could? That woman taught me to be grateful for every single day in my life. That lesson has stuck with me forever.

Every elite athlete and businessperson I have ever worked with has one thing in common—service. They are board members, school ambassadors, golf tournament hosts, and more. They do so because one of the best ways to invest your time comes through service. When you serve other people, you learn more than you could ever imagine.

How do you serve? Where can you serve? Who will you serve?

TRAVEL

Another great way to invest your time is through travel. When you travel, you learn things you never would have known. You never waste time when you travel to a new place. The places you travel never leave you. How do you know what you want to do if you have never seen other people doing it? In Spain, their afternoons include a siesta. Maybe you look at that tradition and think, "That's the way to live life." Maybe you see that and invest your time earlier in the day so you can have some time off in the afternoon, so you can pick up your kids from school. Or maybe you travel to a conference where you learn from leaders in your field.

You can never lose time in educating yourself, whether that education comes from school, podcasts, speakers, events, workshops, or, heck, even trying something new. The most successful people around you are always learning. In the twenty-four weeks it takes to win a Super Bowl, you learn every single week. At no point in that journey do you say, "I know everything. I know what I need to know. We're going to win." It does not work like that. You have to be open to continue learning every-where you go.

HARD WORK PAYS OFF

When we won the Super Bowl, I could not tell you if it was running eighteen 400s in the dead of summer when I was sixteen, waking up at 8:00 a.m. after high school graduation to train when most kids were hungover, or taking yoga class the week before the Super Bowl that helped me become a champion, but I know that the sum is greater than the parts. I might not be able to pinpoint the one exact thing that made me able to succeed, but I know I invested all that time.

Little time investments add up, and one day, they pay off.

Ask yourself, "Am I wasting my time or investing my time?" Yoga is one way I invest my time. I know I have never wasted a dollar on yoga. Connecting mind and body opens me up to have success the rest of the day. When I practice yoga, I come from a good place and give good energy. What do you do that brings energy and creates space? That's a smart investment of your time.

I missed ten Thanksgivings while in the NFL, and now I will be able to have, God willing, sixty where I eat all day and laugh with family. When you invest your time, you are going to have to sacrifice something. We do not talk about the sacrifices we make often enough. Too often, we have this expectation that if we put in the time, it will be given back to us.

My longtime trainer, Ted Johnson, says it best: "The best athletes have zero expectations regarding the work they put in. The worst athletes are the ones who think the game or someone owes them something for their hard work."

Sacrifice is part of the game. Sometimes you are going to have to make them in order to invest your time properly. Work weekends. Work holidays. Create the willingness and space to say, "I work weekends. I work nights. Sometimes I work holidays, so I can take thirty holidays off in a row."

By learning how to invest and value your time, you master your time. When you are the master of how you spend your time, you will begin to reach goals that felt impossible only months before.

To strengthen your mindset around investing your time, I want you to consider these questions.

Do the places you are investing your time fit into your goals?

Are you investing your time in ways that align with your goals?

What are your priorities?

Where do you feel the most value when you spend your time?

What do you like spending your time doing?

Once you have that figured out, ask yourself whether you could be doing more. Could you be working harder, digging longer? I have had to answer that question, and I did not like the answer. When I was a rookie in the NFL,

I knew I could come to work earlier. But I really did not want to. I could stay later. But I really did not want to. I could unplug my Xbox. But I really did not want to. But that is not the point of this work. We all start somewhere. It does not matter what you do or do not like. It matters how you invest your time while working toward a goal.

What are you willing to put in to get better? Can you put in a nickel or dime of time into it? If you are doing something that helps you believe in yourself, that builds your visualization, can you spend five more minutes in that space? Can you shorten a meeting by ten minutes when you are spending time with someone that does not further your goals?

Finally, ask yourself whether you are investing enough time into the one person who makes everything happen. Are you spending enough time with the one person who often gets overlooked on the way to achieving your goals? You.

Are you investing in enough me-time? There is a reason why "me" is part of the word *time*. You need that time to take care of yourself.

You earned it.

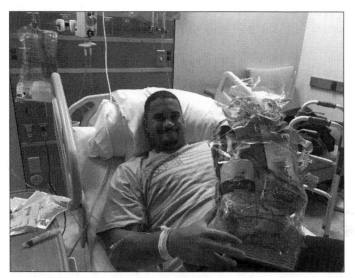

A gift from a coach during one of my many hospital stays over nine surgeries.

A photo of the first time I went fly fishing. I always try new ways to break the routine.

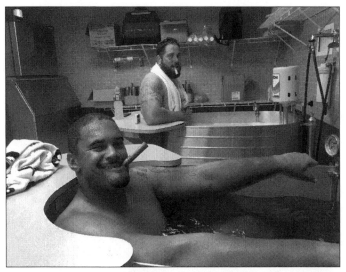

Celebrate every win. At the completion of my tenth training camp, we enjoyed cigars in an ice-cold tub of water. I love this moment in my career.

Before the chaos of a play in Detroit during the World Champion 2015 season.

Pre-Super Bowl flight.

Two-time Super Bowl champion and Hall of Famer Terrell Davis met us in Santa Clara as we landed.

With the trophy.

Post-win celebration.

Tim Cook and me after the confetti at the Super Bowl.

Chris Doernbrack

Celebrating the win.

The offensive line and Peyton the night we received our Super Bowl 50 rings. Each of us in the photo overcame injuries, losses, and doubt to achieve our greatness.

CHAPTER SIX

SUCCESS THROUGH SELF-CARE

"Realize that good time management doesn't mean filling your day with nonstop productivity. To be at your best, you need some downtime. Don't feel bad about napping, watching some TV, or going for a walk."

—WILL DEAN

"Be busy, work hard, but don't become so busy that you cut out other things in life, like family and recreation and hobbies."

—COLIN POWELL

Everyone needs a break. Even the most elite performers. Everyone gets tired of the routine, and taking a break gives you a chance to become excited again about the rest of your journey. In the NFL, that break is called a bye week. Every team gets one. In each of my ten years as a pro, I had three to six days away from the game, away from the struggle, and away from some of the teammates I loved but had grown tired of. Some coaches were better than others and gave us Tuesday to Sunday. Other coaches sucked and gave us Thursday to Sunday. Either way, it was a necessary break. We were pushed to our limits in training and practices.

Interestingly enough, in the NFL, success comes down to what you did in your bye week. Did you take care of yourself to rejuvenate your focus, your desire, and your performance? Did you heal? What did you do when your body was beaten, bruised, and exhausted?

You need to ask yourself these same questions. Because we all need a break in the action.

All that belief, digging, perseverance, investment of time and money—whew! Exhausting. So exhausting that if you do not take time daily, weekly, and monthly to check in and nurture yourself, you will burn out. Protecting yourself from burnout comes with the mindset for mastery. You must look out for your needs, and you must master your energy and rejuvenation to perform your very best. You need to smile, laugh, sleep, get away. That is self-care. Self-care gives you the energy to stay the course and persevere. It provides the strength to pick up a shovel and dig. And it gives you the awareness to invest your time.

Self-care propels you physically and mentally into the journey that will become your ultimate success. Self-care can be a vacation, ten minutes of meditation, a massage, reading a book, or volunteer work. Anything that gives you the time and space to focus on your own well-being can be self-care.

Self-care might seem like a woo-woo phenomenon, but it stands as one of the most critical components of your greatness. It does not have to be something spiritual like yoga or meditation. It can be a walk around the block. Time spent building a tool shed. Smoking a cigar. I define self-care as the things you do by yourself that make you laugh. At its core, self-care is taking the time to take care of yourself. You cannot stay on the path to a mindset of mastery if you do not stop and refuel. Cars have to stop for gas. Planes fly on jet fuel. Spaceships need rocket fuel. Even electric vehicles need to recharge. Everything needs a source of energy; yours comes through self-care.

You need this time off. Not only that, **you earned it**. You believed in yourself. You visualized your success. You dug and dug with your shovel. You persevered. You invested your time. You are not hanging out with people who suck. Now you need some self-care. Congratulate yourself.

Love yourself. Spend time alone and do not feel guilty about it.

A self-care routine can be found in every successful person in every field. Einstein walked to work; Steve Jobs meditated. I have had coaches who ate McDonald's breakfast every morning in the parking lot, and others who got foot massages weekly. Whatever your self-care looks like, remember, it is necessary and nothing to be ashamed of.

If you feel embarrassed about taking this time, you are not alone. In the NFL, athletes call self-care body work because they do not want to be honest about how much time and money they spend on their own well-being. I have had teammates who would fly in acupuncturists, chiropractors, masseuses, or tai chi instructors. I even had a teammate who traveled with Silly Putty for his "me-time." You name it, and I have had a teammate who tried it, because they knew how important that *me*-time was to their performance. I know I did. I had to feel as physically good as possible to perform every Sunday. I needed that massage, and I was not afraid to call it self-care. I needed to make sure my back muscles were loose. I needed my hips and quads to release the lactic acid from the previous week. I had to take care of myself, my body. There is a reason why I had three surgeries in my first four years in the NFL and then none over a five-year stretch of my career. The difference was I dedicated myself just as hard to self-care as I did to the rest of my life. I became a pro and finally took care of myself. I started a yoga practice. I learned to breathe better. I meditated. As soon as I started taking care of my body, my injuries went away. I felt better each and every game. Not only did it help me on the field, I became a better friend, husband, and father, all because I felt better.

What do you need?

What can you put on your calendar for self-care?

If you sit at a desk all day, you might need five minutes of neck stretches. If you do manual labor, you might need a long soak in a bathtub full of Epsom salts, or to see a chiropractor regularly. If you are a surgeon or a cop constantly in highly stressful situations, you might need to zone out to music and dance around your kitchen, or speak to a therapist. It does not matter who you are or what you do, you have to take time for yourself to rebuild your belief and willingness to dig.

Use your mindset for mastery to do the things that make you a better person all-around. When you spend time with yourself, you become aware of who you are and what you are feeling. Withdrawing for a little bit of self-care creates knowledge of yourself that allows you not only to perform but to be present everywhere else. You communicate better. You are more aware of the needs of others. You are more aware of your own needs. Self-care allows you to reach success.

Success should not be full of stress. Do not get me wrong; the majority of your time will be stressful. You will be uncomfortable. You might have to use your headlamp to create some space when digging. But when you get out of that moment, you had better drop that shovel and recover for the next dig.

CREATE A SELF-CARE ROUTINE

Ideally, you want to build self-care into every day. You want to do something each day that makes you smile. If you do not know what that is, think about what makes you smile when you are alone. That should be your self-care. That is where you need to be more often. Self-care can start small and build. Like everything, there are levels. There is a bicycle, and then a motorcycle, and then a plane to take you even farther away. There are levels to self-care, too.

You could start with finding five minutes to meditate every day. You could take five minutes to sit in the sun or call a friend. You could walk around the block. Do something small that makes you happy. For me, the small thing

I do is listen to music or read the news, and if I have the time, I listen to a song that makes me smile and laugh. If I can laugh for three minutes on my ride home from work or before a big speech, I knock it out of the park.

I am not the only one. Before any sporting event, you will see your favorite athlete in that very place. The great ones know that even before the big game, they need to do something for themselves.

So do you.

If we do not take time for ourselves, we often resent a portion of what we are doing. We are looking for a way to cut something short so we can get that *me*-time, only to be rude in one meeting or late to another. All because we do not create our opportunity for self-care.

As a parent, if you take time to be alone, away from adulting, you transform your time with your kids into an opportunity instead of a strain. If you are going to your in-laws, take time for yourself before that holiday or event before you serve other people. How much stronger and more present will you be if you take me-time first?

Find the small ways, the medium ways, and the big ways to make that me-time happen. You can find that song you love that makes you dance. You can find that verse in the

Qur'an, Bible, or Torah that brings you joy and fulfillment. Find those small things you can do every day, and then you can start adding bigger self-care moments to your life. Plan for a day off just for the heck of it. Start that sports league at night, join a book club with complete strangers, or sleep in once a week. Figure out what you like and dislike. Figure out what you need. Then make that time for yourself.

Self-care will be personal to you. Yours will be different from mine. Maybe your care will be getting a certain type of food or watching a certain type of movie. Maybe yours will be laughing, spending time alone, or spending time with others. Maybe it will be golfing or mountain biking. I am one for "pool vibes." We get so many days of sunshine in Denver throughout the year that I constantly get a chance to refuel. I love the sun. I like going to the pool. I get some sun for twenty or thirty minutes any day I can, and that becomes my me-time. Then, when I go to work, I ride those pool vibes through a great broadcast, beamin'. When I see my kids and family, I'm smilin' and fully present because I took some time for me.

Part of your self-care should deal with your overall health as well. It can be the easiest thing to overlook, especially when you are working hard. What do you need for your health? Maybe you need to get away from something or eat something different. Maybe sipping a liter of water throughout the day can become a way of taking some time for yourself. Maybe you need to walk twenty minutes a day. Whatever it is, make sure one of your self-care tools contributes to your overall health. A big part of recharging is taking care of your physical body.

After you accomplish something grand, you might need a vacation. A great sales director I know makes sure he takes a cruise once a year. It does not matter what he has going on; that cruise goes on the books. Coaches in the NFL have vacation homes they visit every March. Find those spaces for you. Where can you plan in your self-care?

Whatever your self-care is, you need to make it happen. Put it on your calendar. Block off the time you need and then some. Set a recurring time for it and do not plan anything else during that window. In my current schedule, I take every Monday morning off. My new schedule has no meetings, no coffee talks, nothing on Mondays. Oftentimes, I do not even have a plan for how to spend that time. Plan a bye week for yourself. Plan a weekend where you take a break and enjoy some me-time. Go somewhere new. Eat something new. Learn something new.

SELF-CARE TAKES TIME

Finding the self-care that works for you takes time. When

I needed to relax, people suggested I try acupuncture. The problem with that? Needles stress me the heck out! I will be relaxed going in, and as soon as those pins go in me, I am tense. So for me, acupuncture does not work. That does not mean I would never try acupuncture again; I just do not consider that self-care.

Sometimes you might have to try several different things before you find what works for you. One of my friends lifts weights for his self-care, but for me that is not relaxing. For him, it is.

It takes time to find what you want to do, so be okay with that. You have got to give things a couple of tries. I did not just try one acupuncture session; I tried three or four sessions before I decided it wasn't for me. This comes back to investing your time. You have to invest the time to find out what self-care practices work best for you.

If you have never invested in self-care, expect to feel uncomfortable at first. If you have never spent time alone, you might find it odd. You might feel guilty that you are not spending time on work or with your family. But remember, investing time properly is an important step to mastery. Investing time in refueling yourself with a little self-care will be worth every second. As a rookie, I did not want to spend money on a massage. But if that sixty dollars helped to prevent an injury so that I could make $1 million, then it was worth it.

Self-care is not something to be embarrassed by. No matter what others might think, it is necessary.

When I was on my way to winning a championship, I could care less what anyone thought about my body work. That work kept my muscles, mind, and body ready to battle on the gridiron for sixty minutes. Once I was speaking to a group, and someone asked me what it took to be in the NFL. "You're gonna laugh," I said. "But it's prayer, hard work, and yoga." Everybody laughed, and I did not care. Yoga made me a champion. It has made me a better friend. It has made me a better husband and father. A better person. I find it a critical part of my self-care.

Be confident in your self-care practice. When you are on your time, it does not matter what anyone thinks of it. Be confident in knowing you are procuring your mindset. By simply taking those five, ten, sixty, ninety minutes of self-care, you will be ready to go beyond.

CHAPTER SEVEN

MASTERY EXISTS BEYOND

"I live life at 212. At 212 degrees water boils, becomes steam. That steam can be so powerful it creates power for a locomotive. At 212 degrees you can deliver goods, transport ideas, create the impossible. Too many people live at 211, 210, even 180. Greatness lives at 212. Great leaders, great companies live at 212. I live at 212."

—DR. RICK PEREA

Do not confuse being able to do something with being great at it. No matter how good you become at something, you have the ability to go beyond.

In any given year, there are 1,696 players on NFL rosters. Only fifty-three call themselves champions every year. Those fifty-three go beyond just playing in the NFL. Those champions seek to master every aspect of the game.

Many guys get to the NFL, and that becomes the success they were looking for. Being a pro is enough for them. They do not think about being a champion, and they fail to look for the advantage, the improvement, and the work to go beyond. Their goal is to remain in the league as long as they can. But there are also players who say, "I want to be a part of something great. I want to win something forever." To do that, to get to that place, you must master your craft. You have to go *beyond* your belief in yourself and putting in the shovel and digging. Find deeper depths to dig. Find new areas to believe in yourself.

To get to mastery, move beyond believing in yourself; beyond visualizing your goal; and beyond the initial perseverance, investment of your time, and building self-care. When you look to go beyond, you know you are headed to mastery. Mastery exists beyond everything you have already done. The rocket ship has to start on earth before it gets to space. Mastery comes from building on all these steps of your mindset before you achieve mastery itself.

Mastery comes down to asking, "What *else* can I do?"

To build your mastery, how can you expand your skill?

Can you learn something new? Can you be better at something you did not think was important? Samurai culture has the concept of *kaizen*, meaning small, steady improvement. Can you improve yourself in some small way today, tomorrow, this week, or next?

When you are going for mastery, you are gaining skills that others are unwilling to learn. The Hall of Famers I have played with were often the first ones on the practice field because they wanted to master their crafts. Literally, the best players in the world at their positions continued to work, to improve, and to seek. The best teams I was on embodied this mentality as well. We wanted to do more than just win games. We wanted to do more than just have our group of friends. We wanted to go beyond.

Do you?

Do you want to go beyond? Do you want to reach past your wildest dreams? It is all too easy to reach a goal and decide you are done. Maybe you were promoted, maybe you bought that house, maybe you finished that marathon. Maybe you did all the things you set out to do. All of that is great. But guess what? There is more. You can always go farther.

After I had been released from the Broncos the first time and went back to play for Houston, I played in a Thanksgiving game where we won in overtime. Postgame, I closed my eyes and prayed. When I did, this unexpected feeling came up: *I want more*. Immediately, I felt embarrassed at the feeling. Then I started to understand what "more" meant. It was not a selfish more. It was a desire to create more, to win more, to feel the feeling of achievement more. I had been to a place in my performance that I worked for, that I believed I could attain, but that was not the end. There was more out there for me and more within me. I had been successful, but I had not won a Super Bowl. That was my more. And I knew it was not much farther to get there.

When you have that wild feeling that you are capable of more, you have found the moment where you create mastery.

KEEP LEARNING

Mastering your craft means finding all the little ways you can learn more. The more skills you gain, the more you can achieve. If you are going after mastery, you are always learning. And there is always value that somebody can give you, whether you agree with it or not. Find the opportunity to try something new. Build a mindset that seeks opportunity and values others' contributions.

When I first made it to the NFL, my coaches wanted me

to try new things. There were different training methods. New footwork, new plays to learn, new lifts to complete. I thought I knew it all. So I paid lip service. I told them I would do it. I told them I would learn the new footwork. But I did not do it. In my head, I thought I knew what I was doing, and they just had to get on my level. I had overcome injuries. I believed in myself and was willing to work. I had invested my time. I did well. I did not know my coaches and teammates knew I was paying lip service. I had yet to figure out that when you are a part of a team and you lie, you are only lying to yourself.

Be open to others' opinions, feedback, and coaching. Seek out new mentors. In mastery, your mentor might not be someone who's better or greater than you or even in your same field. I can learn about money from a tech entrepreneur who became a millionaire in their twenties the same way I can learn from a former football player. Every president has relied upon counsel and advice from previous presidents. Your mentor does not have to be someone above you. They just have to provide you with a new skill, a new perspective, or a new approach.

Sometimes the best small improvements come from areas outside of your life and your goals. You will find the most amazing skills outside of where your goals are set. Things that seem to have nothing to do with one another will be connected with your willingness to build the skill and bring it to mastery.

MASTERY FOR YOU

In athletics, mastery goes beyond the ability to succeed and be successful. You can become the best quarterback or tackle, and then learn to deceive someone into thinking you are making a run play when, in fact, you are throwing a touchdown to win the game. That difference is mastery. A pitcher can throw a changeup, when it really looks like a fastball. Mastery. Muhammad Ali made George Foreman think he was losing the Rumble in the Jungle, and then in the eighth round, he knocked him out. Mastery. In chess, they might not know what you are doing until you win the game. Mastery.

In business, mastery means being strategic and finding the wins that others are missing. When the iPod first came out, there were other products similar to it on the market, such as Microsoft Zoom and others. Apple went beyond the product and designed better customer use. We have gone beyond the iPod now, but everyone remembers it because it was revolutionary. Apple and its teams dedicated themselves to mastery, and now we have the iPhone and the iPad. Apple went beyond the product and looked to master the aspects others did not care about.

Mastery operates on a completely different plane of performance—one that seeks the unseen and then embraces the path to be the best. The difference between being the best comes with a tiny fraction of a difference.

When I played with one future Hall-of-Fame quarterback and we would get a first down, he would say, "Aw, but you know we could have run that better. We could have gotten twelve yards instead of ten."

At first, you would hear some of us say, "Wow, man! Why don't we just appreciate what we've got?"

But our leader was pushing for that fraction of a difference. He saw the unseen opportunity to improve. When you have decided to master something, you have to find the unseen place where you can benefit. In the NFL, you get paid a lot of money. It can be hard to find the problems with your performance when you are cashing a fat check, but you have to keep looking beyond.

You lose so much opportunity by just being happy with where you are. A lot of people are happy with the lowest level of success. They become complacent with success. If you really want to reach beyond your potential and find how successful you can be, when you experience success, look for more. When you reach success, look for something unseen because there you will gain the edge you need for your mastery.

With a mindset for mastery, you push yourself to reach your ultimate goals. When you live your mindset—when you master yourself, time, and effort—people will notice. People will want you to lead. Often, your success will depend on leading others the very same way you have led yourself to mastery.

Ready or not, your mastery will make you a leader.

CHAPTER EIGHT

BECOMING A LEADER

"I've never aspired to be a leader. I have only focused on doing things that I felt were important."

—GINNY GILDER

"Leaders aren't born, they are made. And they are made just like anything else, through hard work. And that's the price we'll have to pay to achieve that goal, or any goal."

—VINCE LOMBARDI

When you have done all the work to reach the mindset of mastery, you become a leader for others around you. You become an example of what it means to believe in yourself, visualize success, and pick up a shovel and dig. By persevering, investing your time wisely, allocating me-time, and being willing to go beyond, you show others how it can be done. Your *I am, I can, I will* attitude becomes noticeable to everyone around you.

Whether you realize it or not, you are starting to become a leader. When you have a mindset for mastery, your mindset finds the unseen victories, and you find yourself in a position to be a leader because of your ideas, products, sales, and success.

You might not notice how much you are leading the pack, how you are making headway, or how you are breaking the current, but those around you will. They will take note. People will start asking questions. They will want to be around you, spend time with you. During my freshman year of college, I arrived on campus in outstanding shape. I ended up playing that year. At the time, I was the third freshman in the history of Notre Dame to play on the offensive line. When we got to the off-season, one of the upperclassmen approached me. He said, "Hey, Ryan, what are you doing for workouts this summer? Can I join you?"

I had this moment where I thought, "You are going to be a senior. What do you want to join me for?" Later, I understood. He had seen that I came into the season in shape, that I had performed well because of how I worked out, and he wanted to be a part of that.

I never thought about becoming a leader; it happened naturally at different times in my life and career. That teammate of mine later went on to win the Most Improved

Player on Offense award. I was leading, even though he was a leader on the team. This happens all the time at top levels of organizations.

LeBron James did not set out to be a leader. He was simply trying to be the best he could be. Then, all of a sudden, he became recognized as the greatest player in the world, and people now look up to him. Steve Jobs was just trying to launch a hardware and software company. Then, all of a sudden, he became the face and spokesperson for one of the largest companies in the world.

When you have the mindset of mastery, you are going to elicit one of two responses in people. Either you will scare the shit out of them, or they will appreciate what you bring and where you are going. Either way, people are going to notice your efforts.

The people who have the first response will not like you. You do not make excuses, you threaten their way of life, you work harder than them, you sound different than them, you fail different than them. You threaten their comfort. They want to live a life of complacency. Not you. You are willing to go beyond. Whether people like you or not does not concern you. Ignore them and pay attention to the others.

The people who appreciate and notice your efforts are

going to be curious. They will notice the belief you have in yourself. They will feel the positive impact of how hard you work to dig, the visualization you do, the me-time you take, and the perseverance you have to stay the course.

When everything you do is in accordance with what you want to accomplish, people will look to you for motivation. They will see how your hard work pays off. They will see that your mindset has you in tune with what you are doing. They begin to understand that there exists a reason behind what you do every day. Though this may take some time on their end, it will happen.

By living your life with a mindset of mastery, you naturally become a leader.

In the NFL, I started staying late to watch film on Wednesdays and Thursdays after practice. No one else did this. In that first week, my teammates' responses were, "What the hell is Ryan doing?" By the third week, a couple of guys stayed with me. They saw that my work to watch film was paying off on the field. They were curious. By the fifth week, there were five or six guys staying late to go over film and ask questions. We all started to work together to be better players.

Eventually, around weeks nine and ten, a couple of the guys stopped staying late. They found their way to study film. For me, staying late worked. For others, they wanted to watch the film at home or in the morning. Either way, they were still doing the work. They discovered what worked for them. As a leader, seeing those guys find a method that helped them dig was one of my happiest moments in the NFL. My work was paying off not just for me but for others too. They would continue those habits long after I was their teammate, and in that way, I helped them become better players. That to me defines being a leader.

When those around you are inspired by your mindset of mastery, you are truly living beyond. You are becoming a leader. To achieve your greatness as a leader, take these six actions with you everywhere you go: leading by example, encouraging others, empowering others, supporting your team, being vulnerable, and stating the goal.

LEAD BY EXAMPLE

Now that you have a mindset for mastery, you can share it with others. You can connect with other people to help them believe in themselves.

Just as you have a choice in how you manage your time and who you spend your time with, as a leader, you have a choice in how you lead. You can choose to jump right in to the tough situations and encourage others.

We all know leaders who say something but do the absolute opposite. They call on you to do something but are unwilling to do it themselves. You might have a boss who prefers you stay late on Fridays when they are out golfing. You might have a colleague who asks for your help on projects but never helps you. Those are bad leaders.

If you want to be a good leader, go beyond just talking the talk. If you are the head of a sales team and your goal is to break the company sales record, you cannot ask everyone else to make five extra cold calls a day while you answer emails and never bring in a new lead. You have to do it, too. If you are a business owner and the market is down, you will lose your company and credibility if you ask others to take a pay cut while you keep your CEO salary. You have to be willing to exemplify the level of commitment you expect others to have. Being a great leader goes beyond leading by example. It includes building each other up as well.

ENGAGEMENT BRINGS EXCELLENCE

You may be good at believing in yourself, but if you are on a team with people who do not believe in themselves, you have a job to do. Make sure you communicate to others that you believe in them. Encourage them to believe in themselves. Talk about the tough changes you had to make. The losers you had to distance yourself from.

Then, when you see their effort for change or their new approach to a problem, give them a high five. Tell them what a great job they have done.

We fail to encourage each other enough. We miss opportunities to say, "Hey, great job." "You've really been working on that. Way to fix it." "That was excellent." "You really saved my ass on that project." But we can. A great leader engages and encourages every opportunity they get.

At the elite levels of competition, and on the path to your greatness, understand that your success depends on the performance of others. Choose to engage as a leader, or you will miss out on the experience and joy of shared success.

A great leader engages with everyone. If a colleague's mother is sick, give them a little slack. If a friend has a tough week at work, offer encouragement. Take them out for coffee. Make sure those around you feel seen and heard. You are all on the same team.

This does not mean you have to be friends with every person you work with, but you do have to show respect. I have had some teammates I could not stand to be in the same room with. There was one guy in particular. If we saw each other outside of the facility, even to this day, we would fight at the drop of a hat. Period. But when we worked together, we were on the same page. Even with other teammates I disliked, I would ask simple questions that did not take much from me, like "How was your day off?" "How was that movie you saw?" "How were those eggs you just ate? I was thinking of getting some too." I engaged because we were on the same team working toward the same goal. If you do not engage, you are choosing to miss an opportunity to connect with those you lead.

As a leader, you ultimately want other people to achieve their own greatness, their own success. You want to see them, smile at them, and connect with them. Recognize those around you. Ask questions. Know what other people's lives are like. Show up at a birthday party, a confirmation, or a graduation party. Go beyond seeing people around you as a means to your goals. See them as individuals.

Often, people refrain from talking about their problems, especially in a new group or in high-performance areas. They will not tell you what is going on in their life. I have never told my teammates when people stole from me. My teammates never told me when their parents died. Rarely do people offer information that affects their every move or their performance. But your job as a leader is to bring that out of them. By creating the space for them to talk about their problems, you connect and show that you care. If you see someone struggling around you, as a leader you need to ask them, "Hey, is everything alright? What's going on outside of work?"

Engage by asking questions they have not asked themselves. "Are you okay after the loss of your mother?" "Are you okay after adopting a child?" "Are you okay coming back from surgery?" A good leader asks to make sure they are on the same page but also to make sure they are engaging personally with the people they depend on for success. Good leaders are open for any topic of conversation. Make yourself available to others. Make it easier for them to talk to you.

One of my coaches would always be in the steam room after practices. Every veteran knew he would be in there after a Wednesday practice. There, we would have natural conversations about our lives outside of football. We would talk about and find a way to laugh through our fears and frustrations. There was no judgment, only time to connect. The funny thing? That coach hated going in the steam room, but he knew that was a way to reach his leaders on their level. This is the kind of scenario I want you to create. Not everyone can have a steam room conversation with people in their office, but the point is to make a personal effort. A leader who engages benefits the entire team working toward a goal.

EMPOWER OTHERS

A great leader values others more than they value personal success. When you value other people's contributions, you acknowledge and engage with others. When your team starts to win, you win. The more you grow as a leader, the more you will notice the importance of teamwork. You will recognize that you cannot do it by yourself. Instead, you will choose to empower others and highlight the efforts of other people.

DeMarcus Ware was one of the best teammates I have ever had. He would often talk with me about how to be successful as a tackle, because he had beaten everyone there was since he was in the league. As a defensive end, he went against tackles all the time. He knew the ropes, and he could see where I could master my craft. One day he said, "Hey, Ryan. I notice in practice you're giving the play away by your back foot." All I could think was, "What back foot?" I had no idea I was giving something away to an opponent. It was a small thing, but DeMarcus's taking the time to help me improve was huge. He did not have to help me during practice. I was not even on his side of the football. But he knew that if we were going to be successful, I needed to make sure I was not tipping my hand when we ran our plays. By him taking that small moment to correct my mistake during practice, I was able to fix it before the game. He wanted to be great, but he wanted the rest of his team to be great, too. He was a captain of our team because of how he engaged and went beyond his performance. He found ways to heighten everybody's performance. He uplifted and encouraged the entire team. He understood the dynamics of the team. He was a great leader.

Your success will rarely be a solo endeavor. When you succeed, you succeed because of the impact of those around you. The higher you go, the more you depend on others. No one scores every point in a game on their own. No president in history won their election solo. In the NFL, I played on an offensive line where it did not matter how great a game I had; four other guys had to have a good game for us to win. In fact, the whole roster of players had to have a good game for the game to be a success. Every touchdown pass depends on a good throw from the quarterback, protection from the offensive line, and the other receivers running routes to create that window. We all depended on each other. We all worked to better each other. And we won because of it.

CREATE THE FOUNDATION

We all have teams we play on. You might not be in the NFL, but you are on a team. Think about your different teams right now. You have an office team. But often, your first team is your family. You cannot be an effective or great leader in your professional life without being a leader in your personal life, too.

The same way you smile and engage at work, you can do at home. When you come home from a long day at the office, you have to put just as much effort into your family as you do your career. If your goal is to be on the top sales team, make the extra calls. Then find what those "extra calls" are for you as a spouse, as a parent. My kids never cared how I played in a game or what a coach said after practice. They cared that I was as happy to see them as they were to see me.

Engage everyone on your team. Support your team. Communicate where you are going and how you see things in five years, ten years, twenty years. Spend one conversation right now talking about expectations with someone who matters to you. Do not let anyone fall behind. Others depend on you, and you depend on them for success.

You alone are not invincible. Sure, you are working toward mastery, but that doesn't mean you have it all figured out. It just means you have a willingness to work toward your wildest dreams. Recognize that you need the strengths of others to become strong yourself.

BE VULNERABLE

During my fourth year in the NFL, I was benched. Demoted because of a play and sent over to be the scout team offense after starting twenty-five games in the NFL.

A guy who I used to play with saw it on the news and called me.

"I know what it's like," he said. "The media is asking if you're injured and you're saying no. Teammates are asking if you're injured and you're saying no. You don't want to tell them you got benched, but that's what happened. I know because I've been there. Just keep working. You'll never know what can happen."

Having that player call me gave me the confidence to keep going and changed my career. I am so thankful he called, because being benched made it extremely hard to find any belief in myself. In that moment, I felt like he was the only person who believed in me. I thought I sucked at my job. But he helped me see that I still had a future in football. This big bad football player was vulnerable with me about his struggles when he faced them. By taking that action, he made losing my job less of a big deal. I started to see it as a frequent occurrence in the NFL, and the effects of losing one's jobs were determined by the actions the player took after the fact. From this experience, I made it a point to do the same and relate my experiences to others that I can see are in tough times.

To be a great leader requires a level of vulnerability. Vulnerability in a leader allows others to relate. When you share your own personal experience with others, they understand that they are not alone. When you are vulnerable and share examples of the tough times, you become human. Whatever example you give in how you overcame those tough times, you will see it in the person you are leading. What a way to create loyalty, performance, and teamwork.

When you see others struggling, what experience can you offer? What wisdom can you share from your own difficult times? How can you be vulnerable enough to lead?

In the NFL, there are three rounds of cuts before you make a team. Before announcing the third-round cuts one time, a coach said to all of us players, "You know what me and these coaches here have in common with you today? We've all been fired. Some of you are about to get fired. I want you to know it's not the end of your story." After hearing those comments, those who were fired did not panic. They did not think, "Man, life's over." Instead, they thought, "That's alright. That coach has been there before, and look what he made of it." That was a leader giving an example of a tough moment others were about to go through.

STATE THE GOAL

"Set the expectation early, and often."

—BILL O'HEARN

In training camp for the Broncos the year we won the Super Bowl, Shannon Sharpe, a Hall of Famer, two-time champion, and former Bronco, came to speak to the team. He was giving a talk on what it takes to be a winning team. He said, "If you're not here to win a championship, get out. There's only one goal on this team." Even though he was not our coach, his sentiment resonated with all of us. He stated the ultimate goal. Here was a champion relating what it took. We all felt we wanted to make it to the championship game, but when he said it aloud, it solidified our desire. Until that moment, we had yet to collectively say it out loud. There were rumblings among us, but to have someone speak our goal into existence for the entire team to hear made the goal clear. It gave us permission to talk about it, to keep reaching for that goal, to *want* to be champions.

As a leader, it is your job to state early and often what you will do and where you will be. If you want to reach that ultimate goal of breaking sales records, then you are going to have to lead. State the goal early and often so your team understands where they are going. Tell them the plan. Encourage them along the way. Give them a scoreboard that shows makes and misses. Let them know it will take more than they have already done to do what you want to accomplish as a group. Believe in them.

State your goals out loud even if they seem far-fetched.

When you state things out loud that seem distant, you give people permission to talk about them and think about them. Too often, leaders are afraid to state their big goals. I had one coach that told us, "Let's try and win ten games and go from there." Not only did we not win ten games, we sucked the whole year. No direction, no goal.

When you lead through these six principles, you become a leader others will follow. Beyond that, with your mindset for mastery not only will you make incredible goals, but others will see how to achieve them as a part of your team. As a leader, you now have one goal—WIN.

You create wins not only for yourself but for those around you. Your mindset for mastery has taken you to the place where it has come time to celebrate. Time to celebrate more than your mindset, more than your achievement, more than reading this page. It is time to...Celebrate. Every. Win.

CHAPTER NINE

CELEBRATE EVERY WIN

"Whenever you get to win, you feel the satisfaction of all of your hard work, all the sacrifices, all the blood, sweat, and tears. It feels right and makes you realize that you are really doing the right thing."

—ABBY WAMBACH

Life will be tough. Building, maintaining, and mastering your mindset will be some of the hardest work you have ever done. Even when you believe in yourself. Even when you say, "*I am, I can, I will.*" Even when you visualize the prize, dig in, and persevere. Even when you make the right investments with your time and you take care of your body and mind. Even when you go beyond and start to lead, you will continue to face obstacle after obstacle.

There exists no perfect path to your goals. Sometimes your heart will break. Sometimes you will not get that promotion you have earned. Sometimes someone else will win the award or finish the race. Yet you still will have made it to that place to be disappointed. You still will have won.

If you are willing to open your eyes, you will find there are wins all around you. The full power of the mindset of mastery changes the way you experience failure forever. Your mindset allows you to keep moving forward with a positive outlook despite setbacks or challenges. Celebrating every win allows you to have fun. It allows you to stay positive and see the progress you are making. When you focus on the positive, you can find the wins in every opportunity.

In the NFL, I sure as hell did not want to go to practice every day. But I looked at those practices as an opportunity to celebrate the fact that I was alive, that I had a J-O-B. I saw it as a chance to celebrate the fact that I could get out of bed, drive to the facility, and run plays and drills. I would celebrate by screaming, "Rock and roll, man!" before, during, and after practice.

I might have dreaded practice some days, but I found a way to celebrate everything. I saw it all as an opportunity to be better. I celebrated being able to practice. I celebrated being able to be pissed off about having to wake up early. I celebrated the opportunity to hate something I had to do like running. After everything I had been through, after everything I had built in, after all the belief I had to have in myself and all the hard work I had to put in to even be allowed to walk out onto that field, I took the opportunity to celebrate. Noticing the small wins that I had every day brought me great joy, great accomplishment. It brought great belief in myself and my abilities. When I walked into the locker room and was able to suit up, it was a good day. When you walk into your office and your key card works, it is a good day. When you find that great parking spot, what a good day. When you can buy the coffee you want without thinking twice, what a great day.

CELEBRATING EVERY DAY

Every day you choose whether to celebrate every action you take or not. Celebration brings you gratitude for what you have. If you look, you can find a win in every moment. Did you wake up this morning? Win. Did you have hot running water in your shower? Win. Did you eat breakfast? Win. How many wins can you celebrate before you leave the house? How many people go without what you already have today?

The next time you buy a cup of coffee, think about what it

took for you to be able to go and get it. You have probably bought your favorite drink a million times, but you have probably never thought about what it took to get there. What have you overcome to be able to buy a coffee? Not just in a day, but overall. To buy that coffee you had to have money. But how did you get the money? You had to have a job. But how did you get the job? Did you go to school? Did you learn a trade? Or maybe the money was a gift from a loved one. To get that coffee you had to go through a lot. Now your morning routine brims with accomplishment. You never just buy a cup of coffee in a morning; you do a hell of a lot more.

That cup of coffee is far more than just the three dollars you have today. It is the remaining three dollars from all the obstacles you have overcome and the choices you have made to enjoy what you want to enjoy. Celebrate that whole journey. Not just today, but every day. I bet you will never look at a cup of coffee the same again.

You picked up a shovel and dug. You were willing to believe in yourself when no one else did. You stayed the course and persevered. Now take that mindset of mastery and use it to appreciate everything you do.

What did it take to be able to take a shower today? What did it take for you to go get that massage for your me-time, or to spend time making music? Whatever it is that makes you smile by yourself, what did you have to do to get to that point?

When you are able to celebrate through all the tough, terrible, shitty times, and you start celebrating wins, you appreciate every single good and bad thing on your journey. You enjoy the process.

In football, we lost games and we won games. But no matter whether we won or lost, we celebrated together because we learned lessons. We knew what it took to get there. It takes a lot to even lose a game in the NFL. Do you know what a team has to go through to be on the field and lose a game in the NFL? How many years of practice? How many injuries every player had to overcome? How many times a guy had been benched or told they were not good enough? How many times players have had to dig in when they were exhausted? Millions of people have played the game of football, but only a small handful have stayed the course to end up in the NFL. That is a win.

Celebrate all your wins. No matter what you do in your personal or professional life, you can find them. You woke up today. Some people did not wake up this morning. You are reading this book. Some people cannot read. You can sing along to your favorite song in the shower. Some people go through life and never hear music.

In my recoveries, celebrating every win was vital. With my toe surgery, I celebrated one victory every week for thirty-two weeks. I had to work to try to gain one degree of movement per week. Some weeks I achieved it, and other weeks I did not. Either way, I celebrated each little win. Every Friday, when I would hit a degree, I would celebrate. "Woo! Alright. One degree closer to getting back to the football field." I would celebrate whether I believed I would make it back to the field or not.

After that specific injury, I had incredible fears about playing again. Incredible fears that I would not be ready in time. That I would never be the player that I had been. That I would never improve. That this was as good as it would get. But I celebrated those degrees, and when I celebrated, I forgot about my self-doubt. I forgot about my fears as I gained gratitude.

What are the wins you can celebrate right now? What are the wins that can help you focus on your abilities? What are the losses that you can learn from? If you are feeling stuck, remember the phrases *I am, I can, I will.* Whether your win is reading one more page in this book, calling somebody to tell them you love them, or advancing your career, when you apply your mindset to all aspects of your life, you have endless possibilities to achieve. And you will. Sooner or later, if you celebrate enough wins, you start seeing your ability versus your fears and doubts.

Even if you do not accomplish everything right away, deny yourself failure. There are lessons to be learned. I did not become a champion until my ninth year in the NFL. However, each year I became better, and I learned something I needed to learn, whether I could admit it or not, over those previous eight years. I experienced achievement on a daily basis because I found the wins that were all around me. I ate breakfast. Win. I got married. Win. I had two children. Wins. I won games. Wins. I recovered from surgeries. Wins.

Find your wins in every day.

FIND THE OPPORTUNITY

With your mindset for mastery, you now find every opportunity. You become grateful for every mistake. You forgive yourself and you learn from it. You write down what you want to fix and you do it. You no longer carry your failures.

When coaches would yell at me about my mistakes as a young player, I would take it personally. I dwelled on them as if they defined me. During my sixth year, I decided to no longer identify with my mistakes. Instead, I decided to be grateful for every mistake I made. I decided to be grateful that I learned then and there so that it would not happen later. When I took this attitude, I could be happy when someone pointed out a mistake in practice so

I could fix it for the game. Forgive yourself and be grateful for mistakes and what they can teach you.

In the NFL, we each received a grade sheet after every game. For every play, we would be awarded a plus or a minus. The day after the game, we would receive this big list of things to work on. Then we would go into a meeting where the coaches would go over every single play we made, right there for everybody to see. They would analyze it out loud in front of everyone. They would tell you, "You did well here, then you did poorly there," because of this or that. Every play of the game was scrutinized.

Some people might see this as a terrible thing, but with my mindset, I *chose* to view these moments as an opportunity to improve. That became something I could celebrate.

I eventually reached a point where I looked forward to the grade sheets. I loved that it did not matter how big or small the win or loss; we all had work to do the next day. We had the opportunity to become better. I celebrated the fact that I made it through another game in the NFL and I had the opportunity to improve.

Believe in your ability to improve. Leave those thoughts of doubts and humiliations behind you. Celebrate your mistakes and know that you are beyond even the worst of your mistakes. Master your mindset by choosing to celebrate every win.

CELEBRATE WITH YOUR TEAM

When you celebrate wins with other people—your team, your family, or your company—you create bonds that obstacles cannot break. You overcome things together. You cannot be brought down by anything. Together, you celebrate those little wins, and that helps keep everyone going. It makes sure everyone has FUN!

Often, teams fail to win because they forget to celebrate. If you are going to be spending time with others, you better know how to celebrate together. If you do not know how to celebrate each other's successes, you will take on the identity of the consistent losses and begin to resent the people around you.

The things I remember most about winning the Super Bowl are the little celebrations we had along the way. Winning the Super Bowl was absolutely up there as one of the best experiences of my life. The back and forth I had with my teammates throughout the season made the celebration that much better. As a team, we celebrated the wins and losses, the mistakes and joys, together. Those celebrations are what I cherish the most about that experience.

Now, I find those little celebrations all around me. Getting coffee. Going to yoga. Spending time with my wife and kids. Traveling. Reading books. There are celebrations in everything because the journey to achieve mastery never ends. Your goals will change. Your life will twist and turn, but there will always be moments you can celebrate.

You now have the mindset of mastery. You now know how to celebrate all the wins. Find them. Celebrate them every day. Celebrate that you learned something in this book. Celebrate that you have read to this point! In fact, let's celebrate that win together. Way to go. Rock and roll! WOO!

CONCLUSION

You are now part of a greater team of people who choose their mindset, and when you choose your mindset, you change more than your surroundings; you improve the world place and productivity. You change more than the relationships you have, and by doing so you choose to change the world.

Your greatness comes down to your choices. At some point, your good will not be good enough. But now you know you can put in the shovel and dig. You can make one improvement in some way, shape, or form, every day. You can do the small things that will have a lasting impact. You can believe in yourself, visualize your success, and push to your beyond.

You can practice achievement and be grateful for all the

moments that led you to this point. You can celebrate every win. You can lead others to their own greatness. You can use *I am, I can, I will* to reach your wildest dreams.

You will still face obstacles; choose your mindset, and you can and you will move beyond. Any time you are down and you feel like it is too hard; any time you feel like you cannot do some of these things; any time you feel like giving up, know that I have been there. I did not believe I could play football after my third back surgery. I did not believe I could become a pro out of college. I had my doubts when I was fired from the Broncos.

Whatever your level of belief at any moment, know that I believe in you. Every successful person you have ever seen or looked up to has chosen their mindset.

You now have the tools to build yourself a mindset that can change the world.

So let's change the world.

ACKNOWLEDGMENTS

All praise and thanks be to God, the Most High, the Irresistible, the one who created us and unites us all. Thank you to my wife, Jamie, for bringing joy, understanding, and laughter to every day of my life since we met. Thank you to my family. Mom, Dad, you both taught me so much about achievement and mindset from an early age. Kendra and Sam, I cannot wait to see how you change this world. You are the best siblings a brother has ever had. To Betty Wilcox, Carole Wilcox, the Harris Family, Nana, and Papa, you continue to exemplify class and intelligence in every conversation and action you take. The Gruncles. My first football memories were playing "fumble" between the Thanksgiving games at 2820. Thank you for all the memories before and after. Thank you to my Emerson and Wilcox family. Tyler, there are no words for the brotherhood you have blessed me with.

Thank you, love you. Thank you, Adrienne and Lauren Johnson. Thank you, Carlson Family, what a journey; thank you for everything. Thank you, Outlawx, Howe, Salas, and Williams families. Mary Anderson, you continue to be one of the greatest heroines in my life, thank you. To Michael and Mary Daugherty, thank you for keeping me on track and teaching me about life beyond football. Nehwr, thank you for teaching me so much about life and my abilities. May you and all your love find a joyful peace as the future unfolds. Jamal, my twin brother, may you be blessed for your brotherhood, laughs, and restaurant recommendations. TBP. Omar Suleiman, Husain and Hamza Abdullah, Ashab Network, Tariq, the Triplets, Ibtihaj, Samir, Aja, Tone Trump, you are all an inspiration and family to me. Thank you for your love, support, fellowship, and laughs. To my friends and family in St. Paul—Justin, Pat, Chad, Tommy, Noel, Marcus, Big Ash, Seth—you guys have been brothers from the beginning. Thank you, Greg and Elizabeth; the village is strong! Todd Ross, my brother, thank you for all your support. To the Phat Pack; the Bullpen; Astronauts on "The Rocket Ship;" Cory Martin; the Denver crew; the cigar club of Sean, Jerry, Greg, J.P., and others; the Hazardous Hombres; Andrew Diggins; Pat Reis, thank you.

Michael Bonner, Ben Birk, Ken Highfill, Nate Kreckman, Andy Seth, Erin Weed, Josh Dorkin, Reggie Brooks, each of you have had a profound impact on my life in many ways. Thank you.

Ted Johnson, Performance Athletix, you were one of the first to believe in my abilities, something I will never forget. You were there for every injury, the good, the great, and everything in between. Marc Montoya, thank you for training me as a champion. To Dr. Josh Sandell, you saved my career. I am eternally grateful for your involvement and the diversity you bring to my life. Dr. Vitanze, thank you for teaching me how to take care of my body as a pro. Wade Brinkman, you are the man. Loren Landow, you were the missing link I needed; thank you for all the work. Robert Rudelic, I am nowhere in the NFL without your guidance, presence, and time. One of the greatest joys in my career was celebrating the Super Bowl with our families. YES! Dr. Rick Perea, you were integral in my leap to champion. Thank you, looking forward to the future. Dr. John Kerby, you kept me on my feet. Thank you for everything and for the future everything.

Thank you to all my former teammates for the lessons and laughs. Thank you, Kupaloop, Ryan, Brandon/Melvin, Tfa, B. Brooks, Brady, Eric D., Eric O., Lou, Evan, Mike, Matt P., Max, Zane, Kyle, Puggs, Dwalk, Cody, Ramon, and Al for the travels, conversations, working alongside me, laughing, and pushing me. The Salty Crew, SB50

Brothers, you raise the bar everywhere you go. Happy I could be part of the grind.

Thank you, Notre Dame, the NFL, Nike, Eugene Parker, Paul Lawrence, Shelly, Rebecca Otto, and APC.

Thank you, Flip, Harry, Kenny, Rodger, and all the members of the equipment staffs throughout the years; you guys do not get paid enough.

Thank you to the medical staffs for putting me back together again, and again, and again, as much as you could.

Thank you to the coaches who made me a better man and player: Coach Kallok, Willingham, Weis, Kubes, Shanny, Rodger, Luke, Coach T, Reid, Mudd, the Scanlan brothers, Hitch, Bisch, Latts, Clancy, Rico, Denbrock, McDonell, Andy Heck, and Munch. You guys are the absolute best a player could ask to learn from and play for.

If I missed anyone, thank you, love you, see you soon.

About the Author

RYAN HARRIS was a four-year starter for the Fighting Irish, graduating from the University of Notre Dame with a degree in political science and a degree in economics and policy. He went on to start in seventy games with four different NFL teams, including all nineteen of the Super Bowl 50 season. Today, you can catch Ryan live on Sports Radio and television as he provides analysis for Altitude sports, Notre Dame, and others. He also regularly speaks to organizations about the mindset of mastery, financial literacy, and leadership. Ryan lives with his wife and two kids in Denver.

Manufactured by Amazon.ca
Bolton, ON